Empaths

AT THE EDGE:

Heal Your Soul, Awaken Your Intuition,
and Become a Mighty Force of Compassion

By Ashley Kay Andy

Paperback ISBN: 978-0-578-74920-4

First paperback edition September 2020.

Photographs by Jenny Meyer

Printed by Ashley Kay Andy
AshleyKayAndy.com

This book is dedicated to my Uncle Bill whose unwavering love, encouragement and support has transcended his physical lifetime on Earth.

Thanks and love to my daughter and husband, who've inspired me to live my life to the fullest. To my loving parents and siblings, who have guided me and taught me many lessons. To Mrs. Vint, who fostered the gift of creative expression through writing and encouraged the exploration of life through the reading of books. To Shimen, who introduced me to the beautiful art of energy healing and kindly taught my inquisitive mind. To Jenny, whose creative inspiration and soul work reaches far beyond her camera magic.

And to each and every body, mind, and soul who has trusted me to help them heal… whether on my hands-on healing table, through meditation videos, a connection on Instagram, or in my workshops and retreats. May you grow to love and appreciate your gift of sensitivity, embrace your empathic abilities, and live a healthy, peaceful and fulfilled life.

CONTENTS

PREFACE

Welcome, friend. You're holding a book, a guide, a resource filled with messages from myself and beyond for the empaths in this world that are at the edge.

Perhaps you feel you're at the edge of losing it... your sanity, your feelings of security, your emotional handle on the world around you. But if you aren't aware of it yet, you're on the edge of much more.

The edge of diving deeply into a life fulfilled with love, peace, and service. The edge of embracing your inner empathic abilities and gifts. The edge of realizing your potential and the pure GOOD you are here to do on this planet.

You're waking up. You fully understand that there is something important brimming and that you are here for a big purpose. You are becoming aware that you have some special gifts... ones that often make you feel overwhelmed or alone because my friend, you are UNIQUE. It is estimated that only about 15-20% of the population are highly intuitive empaths, and while we all have the ability to tap into our empathic powers, YOU are one of the gifted.

Along with this realization and awakening comes resistance

and fear. Imagine for a moment that you are on the edge of a cliff, hanging miles high above the ground below. You are guided to jump, to leap off the safety and security of the cliff's edge. Every intuitive instinct is guiding you to leap, reassuring you of safety and protection… to just do it! Meanwhile, every ego-driven preservation instinct is fighting tooth and nail against your intuition. That part, led by your busy mind and not your soul, is simply trying to follow every evolutionary guide ingrained within you to keep you safe and living. If you live your life on that cliff you may stay living but will you truly be ALIVE?

This book is written as a guide to the empaths at the edge from one who has been there. One who teetered and resisted for too long. I am here to teach, encourage, and uplift as you leap into the unknown. Because friend, only when you take that leap will you discover the beautiful strength of your wings and the unwavering support of the Universe.

CHAPTER ONE:

WHAT IS AN EMPATH?

When I first discovered the meaning of this word "empath" and that it went beyond simply having empathy, my entire world shifted. I wasn't alone! It was reassuring to discover there were others out there like me, highly sensitive and empowered to utilize their unique abilities to better their life and be of service to others. If you look up the term in the dictionary you'll find empath to be described as, "a person with the paranormal ability to apprehend the mental or emotional state of another individual". In this case the word "paranormal" can be described as beyond normal... an area of existence beyond the scope of "normal" scientific understanding. Just as the world was once widely understood to be flat by the leading scientists and scholars of the day, there is much yet to be understood about intuitive gifts. Your empathic abilities transcend the average levels of empathy and allow you to understand the world in a beautiful light... a light illuminated by the heart.

Much like many reading this book, as soon as I reached

school age I felt different. It seemed to me that I never truly fit in with my peers and that many social constructs or obligations seemed to be frivolous and a waste of time. Despite having meaningful friendships throughout my life and a loving family, I still felt as though I wasn't like everybody else and believed that I didn't fully belong here. When you're young, being different doesn't always feel good.

Your goal as a young child, teenager, and even young adult is to "fit in" with your peers. The need to be accepted is a basic human instinct that allowed earlier humans to survive together within a group. We needed what we considered to be the more dominant individual or group to like us. We, as human beings, subconsciously alter how we communicate and behave depending on who we are interacting with. When you feel emotions as deeply as empaths do, this can come with ease. You understand others' emotions before they say a word and automatically shift to fit within the scope of what you feel would be most accepted. As a child and teenager I was especially concerned about what others thought about me.

When I was a young girl of about ten, I had the exciting outing of picking out some new shoes to start off the school year. August in Northwest Iowa was quite steamy, and my mother allowed me to pick out a pair of sandals along with the typical back-to-school tennis shoes. I stopped in my tracks in front of a lovely little pair of sandals with a slight wedge that had a clear band across the top of the foot, sprinkled with brightly colored flowers. I looked back hesitantly, sure that I would be encouraged to pick something more practical.

Mom admitted with a grin, "Yep, those are definitely 'you', " and I excitedly brought home my new treasures, modeling them for my sister and in front of the mirror as I daydreamed about the upcoming adventures of a new school year. When I proudly wore them to school I was told by a friend that she thought the other girls would make fun of me for them... but not to worry, she had an extra pair in her locker that I could borrow. While I loved those bright flowers and the happiness they brought when gazing down upon them, I certainly didn't want to be teased for them! Perhaps they really were too childish, or attracted too much attention. So away they went, tucked away with sadness and reluctancy into my locker.

Often our empathic gifts and unique abilities are much like that pair of brightly colored sandals. We fear we will be judged for them, or simply lack the confidence and understanding to share them with genuine joy. We avoid standing tall with full knowledge of the unique light we are meant to share, and instead just quietly tuck them away within the depths of our hearts where they remain until we gather the gumption to dust them off again.

That young girl feared judgement and rejection, but she also fully felt and absorbed the feelings of the well-intended friend who was concerned. Those feelings were indistinguishable from my own despite the intuitive guidance from deep within to be my true self. At such a young age I didn't understand why certain people or situations were draining and off-putting, or why I seemed to know what people were going to say before they said it. I didn't know that feeling emotions so intensely can be a beautiful thing when understood, instead of overwhelming. As Dr. Judith Orloff described, empaths are like an "emotional sponge" and instead of absorbing liquid, we absorb the feelings felt by those all around us.

When you uncover why you are the way you are, you can begin peeling back the layers of how you've gotten to this particular place in time. In learning about the traits of an empath, you are given a window into a world of understanding. Before transformation, before positive changes in your life, there has to be a contemplative place of reflecting. This reflection and identifying the life events that relate or "aha!" moments enable you to understand and learn to love being an empath. If you've picked up this book you may already know a bit about the world of empathhood, or perhaps the term is completely new to you. Either way, understanding the traits of an empath means deeper understanding as to how we perceive the world around us and our internal "wiring". While every individual is beautifully unique, there are some common traits that are typically found in empaths. You may recognize a couple of these in yourself… or perhaps you'll find yourself resonating with every item on the list.

1. You're highly sensitive

Have you ever been told (then subsequently told yourself) that you are being "too sensitive"? Often being sensitive is looked upon as a weakness in our society. As a child, I can recall feeling as though something was wrong with me. After all, it seemed nobody around me was so deeply bothered by troubling clips on the news, shows or movies that depicted violence, or touching songs and stories. Books made me cry as I truly felt the emotions of characters within them. Helping on the farm when my dad was stressed made me anxious and overwhelmed, especially if the livestock were agitated or confused. An unkind remark at school felt as painful as a physical blow to my body. I can easily remember mentally telling myself to "toughen up" so others wouldn't see my emotions, feeling as though I wasn't as strong or confident because of my level of sensitivity.

Sure, nobody wants to be the only one crying to the plot of a children's film in a full movie theatre (ahem, been there)... but my friends, "too sensitive" is your SUPERPOWER! Your ability to perceive the emotions of others that may go unnoticed by others is truly a gift as unique as the kindness you are able to show those around you. This gift allows you a beneficial power to brighten others lives as well as your own. If you feel your sensitivity has been overwhelming lately, and are even struggling with the energy to read this book, take a quick break over to Chapter 9 and utilize a tool from the Survive & Thrive kit or listen to a short guided meditation found at ashleykayandy.com

Recenter, refresh, and return.

Journal Prompt: If you've yet to begin the self care and discovery method of journaling, you may want to start as you make your way through this book. Along the way I will be offering journal and meditation prompts that allow you to dig deeper into your empathic abilities, heal, and grow. This doesn't have to be anything fancy, a dollar store composition notebook works just as well as an embossed, leather bound journal. I do recommend writing if you are able, as the process of typing interrupts the flow that a pen to paper provides. Just set your intentions to journal throughout your empath journey and allow the process to guide you.

For your first prompt, I encourage you to write the following list of affirmations.

I am safe to explore my empathic gifts.

I release any negative emotions or energy I am holding onto in this moment.

I am supported by my Higher Self, Mother Earth, God (the omnipotent, loving creator you most deeply resonate with), and the Universe.

My sensitivity is my SUPERPOWER!

I am open to receiving the insight and wisdom my intuition has to offer.

Repeat these affirmations outloud to yourself, perhaps in front of the mirror or as you finish a meditation or prayer time.

2. You absorb other people's emotion

This is where being an empath can feel downright exhausting. It isn't easy to be one who feels the emotions of not only your own experiences, but that of those around you. Imagine for a moment that you are wearing an incredibly powerful set of hearing aids, ones that enable you to hear every conversation going on in a vast event hall room full of people. As interesting as this may be, you really need to focus on the important conversation that you're engaged in with a couple of people close to you. Imagine how much extra energy it would take to focus on your own thoughts and verbal offerings to the conversation over the noise surrounding you.

Being in a room full of people often feels much like this example, only instead of hearing the spoken words reverberating around you, empaths feel the emotions felt by other people in a room and far beyond. Have you ever noticed a difference of your own energy level shifting after discussing something disheartening with someone? This feeling goes beyond holding empathy for a person's situation because you understand what it may feel like... you are truly feeling these emotions with them. It is not that you could imagine being in their shoes, you are feeling what it feels like to actually be in their shoes. It is also likely that wherever an especially strong emotion is present, you are feeling it deeply as well.

A fellow empath shared that she was deeply troubled by the fires occurring in Australia in early 2020 and wept with a heavy heart, thinking about all of the animals unable to survive or injured and suffering. She was consumed by it, and struggled to focus on her college coursework. "I just wish I could fly down there and save them myself!" she exclaimed. It wasn't just her soft heart for animals that was causing her to feel this way. She was truly feeling the deep pain and fear that the animals and humans of the area were experiencing. World tragedies may affect you from around the globe as though they are happening to your own family and thankfully, joyful occurrences are celebrated as well. You may rejoice with a stranger as they learn some uplifting good news or cry tears of happiness as you watch a heart-warming story that happened hundreds of miles away.

Journal Prompt: Can you think of a time where you felt strong feelings that didn't quite make sense with your own situation, or perhaps even recognized that they were coming from outside yourself?

3. You're likely introverted

While many descriptions or imagery depict introverts as those who fear crowds and prefer being at home alone with their book and their cat, this is the more narrow-minded image. This may as well be some introverts' favorite location, but remember that introversion is quite different from having social anxiety or being shy. Decisions to spend your time doing calm, solitary tasks or having meaningful one-on-one interactions is often a more suitable match for your nervous system. While most of the population is found somewhere in the middle of the spectrum between introversion and extroversion, empaths tend to err more on the introverted side. You may feel especially refreshed by a relaxed afternoon on a sunny patio, or working by yourself in the garden. Perhaps you tend to avoid crowded places because of the absorption of energies and emotions, or maybe you just prefer less interaction.

Being introverted means you tend to be focused inward and enjoy activities that are limited to a small handful of people or less. You are often focused on your internal thoughts, feelings, and moods, even allowing them to supersede the events going on around you at times. You may be very self-aware, which is what led you to picking up this book... or perhaps are towards the beginning of your journey, rising into a more aware and awakened existence.

4. You're highly intuitive

If you can recall a time where you felt strongly that you should make a certain decision, but without logical reasons why, you were likely following your intuition. Often referred to as a "gut feeling", we can sense when things feel "right" or not and respond accordingly. We all have intuitive connections of varying degrees, and anyone can improve their connection with their intuition. Empaths naturally are higher on the spectrum when it comes to intuitive gifts, but it's just a matter of tuning in and understanding how to listen to them. Surrendering to your intuitive voice, the one that is directly connected to your Higher Self, Higher Power, and the Universe itself takes practice, but the results are astounding. We will discover more about intuitive gifts and abilities you may possess in Chapter Two (some of which you may be completely unaware you hold within!).

Meditation prompt: Find a comfortable position seated or lying down and take several deep breaths. Mentally place yourself doing something that makes you feel most "you"... that represents your true self and the expression of such. Perhaps when you are creating, moving in a certain way, teaching, or nurturing. Whatever it is, recognize the feeling of unity in your body, mind, and spirit. You feel balanced, centered, and aligned. As you visualize yourself doing this activity that helps you feel this way, pay attention to your emotions as you do so. Are your thoughts guiding you in any way? What is your intuition telling you in regards to this activity?

5. You need alone time

This one was the most challenging for me to recognize personally. I was used to filling my days and evenings with activities, many of which were social activities. When home by myself I needed to be watching a show, playing background music, or talking on the phone. I felt what I now see as a desperate need to fill my alone time with noise. By refusing to give in to peaceful alone time, I didn't have to hear that calm and quiet intuitive voice or feel the heaviness of emotion. Because let's face it… there are times we don't WANT to actually hear it. There are times where it can be downright painful for our ego to hear that intuitive voice. Like when it's telling you that your relationship of many years is not good for your soul. Or that you need to spend less (or no) time with a toxic family member.

Feeling the emotions around us can get overwhelming and we need time to recharge. Time alone allows the stimulus of external "noise" to quiet and enables us to tune into that intuitive voice guiding us in the right direction. If we never make the time to tune into our Higher Self, how are we supposed to recognize her/his voice when we hear it? Allowing yourself to energetically cleanse is as critical for your energy care and protection as showering or bathing regularly is for your physical hygiene. Whether this time is spent in meditation, out in nature, or cuddled up with a good book, time alone is an important part of surviving in the world of empath living.

6. You can become overwhelmed in intimate relationships

Intimate relationships are described as such for a reason. These are the people you are closest to and allow you to grow close to them as well. These can include your close family members, friends, and romantic relationships. The closer you are to a person emotionally, the more likely you are to absorb their emotions and let their energetic state affect your own energy. Intimate relationships can often feel stifling… simply because of the amount of feelings involved. You aren't just accounting for your own but you are actively experiencing and seeking to understand that of those you love. It is also common for empaths to hold the other person's emotions in higher regard instead of making sure their own emotional needs are respected. This can lead to imbalanced dynamics within intimate relationships.

Journal prompt: When was the last time you noticed yourself feeling overwhelmed in an intimate relationship? How did you notice those feelings showing themselves? What series of events led to you feeling overwhelmed and did you communicate this feeling or keep it inside? Were boundaries crossed or not yet firmly made in order to protect your emotional space? Write about this experience, allowing your intuition to guide any beneficial changes to be made or boundaries to be discussed.

7. You're likely a target for energy vampires

You, being a source of compassion and understanding, cause people to naturally gravitate toward you. You are likely to fully listen to their stories, and as we do, empathize with their pain and struggles. While this is your gift that is made to be shared, sometimes sharing it with the wrong people can become incredibly draining and frustrating. These people are nicknamed "energy vampires" because that is precisely what it feels like. They are often well intended, though sometimes truly toxic individuals, that are drawn to you for the right reasons... your light. They then latch on and instead of feeling fueled by helping others, with them you feel thoroughly drained and depleted. They either aren't ready to or simply refuse to do their own inner work and work on emotional growth. Instead they use your light for temporary relieving of their pain or struggles, only to keep coming back for more without learning how to be energetically self-sufficient. Many times these people aren't even aware they are doing so, because they are wrapped up in their own story... but the most dangerous are aware.

Unfortunately, there are some darker energy individuals of lower vibration that use your light, your overly compassionate heart and kindness to prey upon. These are the abusive individuals, master manipulators, the narcissists, and the deeply codependent. It is a sad truth that highly empathic individuals attempt to rescue these types of individuals, often despite warning signs.

8. You are replenished in nature

The earth grounds you in a way that surpasses most, and you are deeply connected to the natural world. We, as human beings, ARE nature... we don't just spend time within it. Your time outdoors isn't optional, it is necessary for your emotional, mental, and energetic health. Even five to ten minutes outdoors among the trees, living beings, and water is refreshing and calming to your active nervous system. You may even feel a special connection to certain beings in nature or are able to understand their needs.

The earth around us is as replenished by your presence as we are by experiencing it. Empaths rising and stepping into our power is what will lead to a shift in how we care for our environment. After all, empaths can feel the emotions and energy of more than just people. When we feel particularly affected by a natural disaster, pollution crisis, or endangered species, we are able to translate to others how our Mother Earth is feeling and inspire action. This helps to solidify the continued existence of a beautiful natural world to live within, be replenished by, appreciate, and care for as the generations continue on.

Meditation Prompt: Unless the weather is quite severe, take 15 minutes (or more) to breathe deeply outdoors. Invoke all senses as you simply return to being a part of the natural world. Allow thoughts to come and go like a light breeze through the trees. Rediscover a place where you were fully able to be present in the beauty found all around you. Relax as you envision this feeling loosen and soften your muscles, letting your joints stretch out gently and feeling the elements all around you. Listen to nature all around you.. does it have a message for you?

Journal your reflections if you wish.

9. You have highly tuned senses

While the wording is similar, this trait is actually quite different from being highly sensitive. This demonstrates that our senses themselves (or one in particular) are likely sharper than the average. You may notice a higher sensitivity to a particular type of stimuli, such as a certain type of music agitating your sense of hearing... or the volume of sound seeming louder than those around you. Perhaps strong (especially unnatural) smells cause you to experience headaches or nausea. For example, if I consume too much of a scent or flavor that is unnatural... a highly fragranced or artificially flavored item, I feel out of alignment, unbalanced, and often sick all over. Achy joints, headaches, fatigue were felt intensely as my body and highly sensitive nervous system tried to process these toxins.

You are able to perceive things others may not, which can make life feel like a more intense experience. It also is a beautiful gift, enabling you to connect and interact with life around you on a deeper level. You may be able to pick up on the beautiful occurrences all around you that may go unnoticed for others, such as the intensity in color of the sunset or the particular joy of a songbird.

10. You have a huge heart, but sometimes give too much

Empaths tend to overextend themselves emotionally, caring for others until they are depleted themselves. It is important to first make sure our cup is filled before scrambling around to fill others, and to be mindful of how we feel when being of service. Are you taking part in something that fulfills and inspires you? Or are you sharing your light and love in a way that feels draining and depleting?

Imagine water dripping out of two sources, the first being a large sponge that is filled to capacity. At first, the water cannot help but drip and fall to those seeking its gentle nourishment. The drips continue to slow down until they come to a complete stop… yet those around are still thirsty for the water. So the sponge squeezes and contorts itself unnaturally in order to continue providing others the sustenance they need. It feels that the pressure of knowing there is only so much water to give, holding fear and uncertainty as to the acquisition of more. Before even realizing it, the sponge has drained itself dry of this life-giving nourishment and has nothing left for itself nor others.

On the other hand, the source of water that is the faucet is able to flow steadily as it provides for others. It is fully aware that the life energy of water does not come from it, instead it is simply a vessel in which it pours through. There is plenty for all, and in allowing the water to flow freely, the faucet receives enough for all those in need after first refreshing itself. There is also the knowledge of when to turn the spigot on and most importantly… when to turn it off. In understanding the freedom and joy that comes from being like the faucet instead of the sponge we are able to avoid "burnout" and fatigue from squeezing ourselves too intensely for others.

Journal Prompt: Think of a time you've recently behaved as the sponge. How did you feel about the situation and people involved? How can you be more like a faucet?

I'm sure you had an "aha" moment or two as you read these traits, recognizing ones that particularly apply to you. Perhaps you felt comforted by the knowledge that you are not the only one experiencing life in this highly sensitive way. There is no test or questionnaire as to "how empathic" you are, as we are all in different stages of our journey. Even if only a few of these traits seem to apply to you right now, understand that the others may be in development or simply not apply. Others may seem to make you feel as though this book was written just for you… because guess what, it was! While these traits do not define you, they bring insight and understanding to your inner workings and remind us that we are not alone.

CHAPTER TWO:

YOUR SUPERPOWERS

Consider the history and evolution of humankind. Our verbal communication has grown more complex through time, and technological advances allow us to connect with family and friends face to face from across the world. So much has advanced and progressed from generations before us and yet our deep connection with Mother Nature and one another has lessened while anxiety and depression are rapidly on the rise. What if the complexity of our spoken and written word is actually a representation of disconnection and lack of empathy? If we were able to communicate intuitively and understand the feelings and even thoughts of those around us more, wouldn't this be a more efficient and accurate means of communication? There would be less room for our feelings to be lost in translation, and true understanding of emotion could transcend spoken languages.

The possibility of such a world exists, as the experience of empathhood and intuitive gifts is being further investigated, understood, and empowered. In furthering our empathic connection, we are being asked to step forward to use our abilities to connect mankind. As well as being able to feel the emotions of those around you strongly, empaths are the frequent recipients of intuitive, energetic and spiritual gifts that enable us to perceive the world around us in a different light. While not every empath has been provided the tools or understanding to foster these intuitive gifts, every empath has the ability to practice tapping into one or more in order to further your own growth and be of service to others.

TYPES OF INTUITIVE GIFTS

The "Clairs"

Claircognizance is defined as "clear knowing", having a knowledge or understanding of something that you are unable to retrace back to a cognitive origin. One of the most common of the "clairs", it can often feel like a challenge to explain your decisions or feelings to others. You may know you should or shouldn't be going to a certain place at a certain time, or have a feeling that someone is or isn't an individual that you should spend your time with. You may often find yourself saying or even thinking, "I'm not sure why or how... but I just KNOW". When we are surrounded by logical and analytical minds, the need to validate your decisions or experiences to others can feel like quite the burden. It isn't always easy for others to understand your seemingly impulsive decision making methods. After all, how do you explain that you made a decision because you "just knew" it was the thing you should do? Remember that your intuition is looking out for you in a way that no other physical person around you can. By tapping into your intuitive "knowing", you're trusting yourself more deeply than you are depending on others' opinions or judgement. Your soul's plan and the amazing gifts you were given to share are of far higher importance than the thoughts of those who fear or are disconnected from their own.

When I was interviewing for jobs in the jewelry business after moving to South Dakota for my undergraduate studies, I was excited to be continuing on to the next stage in my adventure of young adulthood. After visiting the town and enjoying the feel and beautiful views of Falls Park, I was ecstatic to be offered jobs at all three stores in which I'd interviewed. I felt this only solidified the certainty I felt about moving there. As I was verbally processing my interview experiences in each store to my mother on the phone I explained, "This store seems like it should be the obvious choice. It is a stunning, new store front with the highest quality jewelry and felt like a positive atmosphere among the employees there, from the interactions I was able to witness." I loved everything about the store itself, respected their jewelry quality, and enjoyed the vibes radiating from employees I met while I was there... yet there was something that just didn't seem right. I knew it wasn't the right place for me, but without a reasonable explanation. I recall telling her, "I don't know why... he seems nice and like he runs an well-managed store, I just don't think I can work for this man" (speaking of the manager). My mom reminded me to trust myself and make the decision that I felt was best.

I decided to accept a job at one of the other two jewelry stores and immediately dove into acclimating to their products and store culture as I got to know the employees. A month or two into working there, a few of my new coworkers were discussing the store I almost accepted a job at. One asked the other, "Did you hear...?" The manager I "knew" that I just couldn't work for was being charged with a sexual harassment suit by an employee and two female employees quit around this time.

I had no logical evidence of why I shouldn't work for him. He was professional, looked trustworthy, never demonstrated anything but upstanding behavior, and presented a fair offer. Yet there was something inside of me that knew that this was not a situation in which I felt safe and secure. There is a popular phrase that represents following your intuition well in just three words.

Trust your gut.

While this phrase has been around for quite some time, it has scientific and biological origins. Our digestive system is the only other location in the body in which neurons exist... the same type of neurons located in the brain. When you hear health and food experts discussing the importance of your gut health, you can understand that the connection between the gut and neurological function are related. And like the brain, the gut responds to nervous system stimuli... especially when you are in danger or perceived danger.

In an interview with Oprah, several young women shared their experiences of attempted sexual assault or abduction in order to educate others how to avoid or escape such situations. While every story was unique, there was a common denominator, a cohesive trend across every story shared. It was that every woman interviewed felt or sensed something was wrong immediately before the event occurred. They had a "gut feeling" or moment of claircognizance that told them someone couldn't be trusted or that danger was near. Some women did not have time to react, and others ignored this intuitive "knowing" because of societal conditioning to be courteous and fear of being considered rude.

Whether deciding where to go for lunch or what to do in the middle of a life-or-death situation, tapping into your claircognizance will beneficially impact your life. Of course, even those who possess and have honed this ability just as a carpenter sharpens their tools are not privy to all of the answers all of the time. They are simply able to live a more aligned life, confident that their intuition and divine connection with God and the Universe are continuously present for support and assistance.

Journal Prompt: Take a few moments to recollect a time when you made a decision that didn't make logical sense, but you just knew that was the right thing for you to do. Did following your intuition work out for you? Were you aware you were following your intuitive gift of knowing? Did you meet any resistance from those around you?

On the flip side, can you recall a time in which you had a gut feeling that you did not follow, and understood later that the outcome may have been better had you done so? How did this feel? Did your body, mind, or spirit offer any signs or feelings to guide your decision?

Clairsentience is clear feeling… when you're able to physically or emotionally feel intuitive messages and spiritual guidance. This gift is one commonly found in the world of empathhood, and sounds similar to the definition of an empath. While clairsentience and being an empath overlap in many ways, empaths are able to feel another person's emotional or mental state while clairsentient individuals may also have an ability to receive psychic messages from beyond this dimension. A clairsentient is an empath, while not all empaths have grown the ability of clairsentience. You may be emotionally affected by the feelings of spiritual beings around you, or pick up on the "vibes" of a place you've never been before with ease due to previous happenings in that particular location.

When first explaining my channeled spiritual guidance to clients who were open to receiving it, I found myself using the same phrase. When explaining how I understood their pain, emotional challenges, or areas of potential growth I consistently said, "I feel…". My clairsentient abilities were allowing my clients to reach a deeper avenue for growth simply because of what I was feeling. I did not hear direction and was yet to receive visual guidance, I simply felt an intuitive message coming through or felt an area in which I could provide healing, guidance, or reassurance.

Clairvoyance is clear seeing, the ability to have visual representations of intuitive guidance or information, if even just for a quick moment. This visual experience can differ from what we physically see with our eyes (though not always) and is often thought of as seeing from the mind's eye. A vision, a dream, a person's energy referred to as an aura, or seeing a spiritual presence that is not present in the physical world are all examples of clairvoyance.

While clairvoyance was not the first intuitive gift for me to awaken to, it was a powerful one. When performing a hands-on healing session with a client in which we were (unknowingly at the time) bringing childhood trauma to the surface, I had my eyes relaxed and partially closed as I was "in the zone" channeling the healing energy of Reiki. I had an image flash before me, one of a young boy joyfully running through an open field with a bird dog alongside him. It was a beautifully sunny summer day and the purity of bliss this young boy was feeling was touching to me. I could sense the freedom and genuine pleasure he was feeling in simply being himself.

He was deeply touched and healed by the session, and remarked with his amazement as to how much the unique combination of energy work and massage therapy were healing deep emotional wounds from his childhood. I hesitated to do so but felt it may be beneficial, so I tentatively shared this imagery with my client. His eyes widened and smiled in disbelief as he recollected an experience of running around with his family's dog (the same breed of which I visualized) when his uncle would bring the dog over to hunt. In a later message he asked, "How old do you believe the boy you saw was?" I responded, to which he shared that he felt as though God had helped to heal his inner child up to about that age and recognized that he had more work to do in order to continue opening his heart and moving forward in his life the way in which he was intended.

Some empaths with clairvoyant abilities are able to see energetic frequencies, sometimes even sensing the energies of spiritual beings no longer in the physical realm. When my clairvoyant abilities began to grow, I would see the natural world differently. I would often see rainbow colored, geometric patterns along the ground or surrounding trees, and could visually observe when the energetic pattern was disrupted. A friend of mine is able to see the presence of spirits who have crossed over, and another is able to see the auras of people they place their focus upon.

Meditation Prompt: With your eyes closed and after taking several deep and relaxing breaths, focus on a particular place of beauty and ease. You may choose to reminisce on a vacation spot, the home you grew up in, or other location you have visited, or perhaps a place you've only dreamt about. As you mentally place yourself in this location, breathe even more deeply and experience what your senses are picking up on. What smells and sounds are present? Are there any flavors or feelings associated with this place? Then, as though there is a projector casting an image out from your third eye, allow yourself to visualize every detail about the scenery. What colors and living beings do you see? How is the light falling upon the objects around you? Continue diving more deeply into the visual aspect of this meditation, allowing yourself to be deeply relaxed and supported by this mini-vacation to your happy place. You can revisit this place often, or choose to visualize different places of clairvoyant tranquility. The more you practice doing so, the more the ability to obtain imagery from other people or spirit is likely to grow.

Clairaudience is known as clear hearing. Some with this ability are able to hear others' thoughts and emotions as clearly as if they were speaking out loud. If you're an empath with the gift of clairaudience who experiences it as such, you likely know it and have asked, "What did you just say?" only to hear them say they hadn't spoken so much as a word. Other clairaudient empaths hear messages as though they are the voice of their own thoughts. These may take longer to discover that they truly are receiving a message from outside of themself, as it is easy to excuse your thoughts away. One important question to ask when you suspect you may be hearing a message is the suddenness of the thought itself. If a completely unrelated and seemingly random thought pops into your head that does not follow your existing train of thought, nor was it stimulated by something you sensed in the physical world, it is likely a clairaudient message.

Clairalience (clear smelling) and clairgustance (clear tasting) are the more rare of the "Clairs" and are as related as the physical sense of smell and taste. Often, yet not always, when a person experiences one, they also have a tendency toward the other as well. Perhaps you spontaneously smell your friend's favorite flower at a time when they could really use your guidance and support or have the taste of your grandmother's prized cookies randomly appear on your tongue when her spirit is near. These senses are tied closely to memories, and nothing quite takes us back to a certain place in time like scents and flavors… making them wonderfully identifiable communication tools from our intuition or spiritual visitors.

Psychometry is the ability to pick up on emotions or associations from a physical object, simply by touching it. If you have psychometric abilities, you may be comforted by or experience negative emotions when thrift shopping… not necessarily because of your own feelings about the object, but because you are picking up on the energy of the previous owner.

When my daughter was two, she experienced a strong psychometric reaction that made my jaw drop. We had lost our beloved dog months prior and were seeking a new canine companion that she could grow up with. I first wanted to look at the local humane society, where we met a lovable dog we decided to take for a walk around the grounds in order for me to assess his behavior and tolerance of a toddler. It was late winter and snow still covered the grounds. We tread carefully around to the back of the shelter beside a line of empty kennels used during the warmer months or for shorter time periods. My daughter on one side of me and the dog on the other, I turned down for a moment to praise the sweet fella for being such a good dog. In those few seconds as my attention was fully on the dog, I heard my daughter let out a blood-curdling scream like I'd never heard before. I feared she was severely injured but couldn't understand how something traumatic could occur so quickly. As I immediately turned to her, she was now standing alone in the middle of one of the open outdoor kennels, still screaming and crying hysterically. I picked her up, noticing that she did not appear to be injured, and stepped outside the kennel where she began to slowly calm back down. Still sobbing, I encouraged her to take a few deep breaths and tell me what was wrong. Between jagged and tearful breaths she told me, "The doggy. The doggy scared. The doggy scared." and began crying all over again. She was clearly not referring to the calm and content dog on my other side, and was gesturing back to the empty kennels. At that moment I realized that my daughter is not only highly intuitive, but has the gift of psychometry.

For many empaths, this ability first shows itself when using, wearing, or borrowing someone else's items. You may notice yourself feeling differently upon wearing a hand-me-down piece of clothing, or picking up on the energy of those who spent time on that lightly used furniture you found at a garage sale. Some feel overwhelmed by the feelings brought about from a piece of heirloom jewelry or when holding a book that first belonged to someone else. On the other hand, this gift allows one to understand others in an interesting way. You may be able to learn about a departed ancestor's life or understand a friend's experience in a way otherwise unknown. Sometimes a brand new item holds negative energy if made unethically or in an unhappy environment. If this is something that you've noticed affecting you negatively, you may wish to use sage or palo santo to cleanse the energy of items (for a tutorial of this process visit Chapter Ten).

Animal communication is another intuitive ability that can include all of the "Clair" gifts. Intuitive communication with animals is no different than intuitive communication with people, except for our reliance on changed behaviors or owner validation of our findings. Animals are naturally intuitive communicators and often use audible messages of sound as a last resort.

As a child I recall being able to communicate quite clearly with animals. Growing up on the farm, I was blessed with many daily opportunities to interact with animals… from farm cats to our dog, to cattle, birds, and horses. The earliest clear memory of this I remember was with a cat mama that I was especially fond of. I'd built relationships with all of the family farm cats, and had a special closeness with a few of them. She was one of my favorites, and she enjoyed that I knew exactly how and where to rub her favorite spots. I felt her excitement and also fatigue, as her belly grew larger and larger. When she seemed to be twice as round as she was tall, we knew it wouldn't be long before her kittens made their appearance. Farm cats give birth to their litters in some pretty peculiar places. We'd found previous litters nestled in the hay barn as one may expect from childhood picture books, but also in unique (and often unsafe) locations such as the seat of the skid loader or the back corner of a cattle shed.

I was likely about 4 years old and it was late spring. We knew that sweet mama cat gave birth to her babies somewhere hidden on the farm, but we had yet to stumble upon them. One sunny day I remember her telling me to wait in the shade of our front yard tree, for she would be right back. I did so as she trotted down toward the old corn crib beyond the cattle yard. I trustingly did as she'd asked and played in the sweet smelling grass and clover as I waited. She returned a few minutes later carrying a kitten in her mouth and dropped her precious ball of mewing fluff into my lap. I can remember her telling me to take care of her little one, and that she would be back again in a minute. Sure enough, she returned with another kitten… and then another until she had all of her sweet little babies with me under the protection of that old shade tree.

As you can imagine, this felt quite magical, though I didn't think it to be out of the ordinary then. This was simply my normal. Before going off to Kindergarten I remember having a lengthy discussion with my favorite cat, "Tigger". He was a striped male who I thought of as having grandfatherly love for me. I was excitedly getting ready for school but was concerned that my animal friends would miss all of our play time together. After all, nobody else was there to talk to them the way I did! I took Tigger (led simply by unspoken suggestion) for a walk between the long line of evergreen trees that felt like an expansive wood to me. I explained to him that I was heading off to school and that I wouldn't be around to play as much. He knowingly reassured me that it was time for me to go and learn, making new friends and loving them just as much... and that he would be here when I got off the school bus. Sure enough, for much of the school year as I can recall, he was there waiting for me when I returned from the school day, excitedly running to show Mom and Dad what I'd made or done that day. As I grew, I quickly learned that talking to animals was considered, "pretend, imaginary play" that was only for little kids. As with many young empaths, my ability to hear and communicate with animals intuitively recessed as I got older though I was always considered the "animal person" of the family. Through working to strengthen my intuitive muscles, I've been able to gradually reawaken these abilities with patience and persistence.

Some have awakened this intuitive ability and are able to receive messages from the animal world on a regular business. An intuitive friend was visiting my home and both our dog and cat gravitated to her instantly. She asked if this room was where I did my hands-on healing sessions. I explained that no, I'd actually only done two or three sessions in that room. "Hmm... " she said, sounding puzzled. "He (the cat) told me he loves when you do your energy work in this room."

Confused at first and feeling she must be mistaken, I soon gained clarity as what she had understood. While that had not been the location of my client healing sessions, I regularly practiced yoga in that very location. Our cat could be sleeping in the other room and as soon as I would begin my yoga flow, he would run to join me while purring with excitement. I chuckled with the accuracy of her communication with him, and the message he chose to share.

Journal prompt: Think of a time when you felt especially connected with an animal, perhaps felt a special bond or even noticed yourself understanding its thoughts or needs. Write about the details of this experience and the communication you may have received or felt the animal was trying to share.

Spiritual Communication involves receiving messages from and being able to communicate with others through energy transfer. This involves receiving messages from your higher power as well as communicating with those who have crossed over and are no longer in the physical realm. Before delving too deeply into communication, let's break down the terminology. When I mention "spirit" I am referring to the energetic body that houses our soul… part of the mind, body, spirit triad that makes up who you are as a person. While the term "spiritual" may conjure up an image of some New Age hippie with dreads and feathers in their hair or make your devoutly church-going grandmother shake her head, the meaning of the word is one of unification instead of separation. Defined, spiritual means "relating to or affecting the human spirit or soul as opposed to material or physical things". Living a spiritual life is not demonstrated by your regular attendance in a church pew or mosque. It cannot be defined by the number of mantras chanted or prayers spoken.

Religion can be a beautiful thing. It can form a sense of community and help to foster a faith in people that changes lives for the better. Unfortunately, it also has the power to create division, encourage separation, and create an illusion of better-than and less-than. While religious people may be spiritual, spiritual people are not always religious. Spirituality transcends the constructs found within the rigidity of religion, and one does not need to practice a particular religion to live a spiritual life rooted in peace and love.

Spirituality does, however, require an openness in heart and mind as well as faith in the certainty of more than physically perceivable in this dimension. As we remain open to interacting on a soul level, we honor our true selves while holding the belief that others have the right to be truly seen, beyond their physical presence. The journey of an empath requires openness to having new ways of being shown to you and seeking understanding without judgement. As we grow to trust in a power greater than ourselves, we allow the ego to sit back and live from a heart-centered place of love. Whether your faith lies in the Universe, God, Mother Nature, Gaia, or beyond, understanding that we are simply a conduit for divine energy to flow through us opens doors beyond our imagination.

I grew up in a Catholic family, with my compassionate mother having taught religious education for over twenty years. As a young girl of about ten or eleven, church at St. Mary's felt like an exciting family outing. We didn't venture to Storm Lake often, only for attending church, gymnastics practice, and if we needed something from the only supermarket store within a forty-five mile radius. Getting to wear my fancy clothes to people-watch for an hour was alright with me! Though I knew I was supposed to pay attention to the priest's sermon, I would often lose interest and find myself staring at families surrounding me, imagining what their lives and relationships with one another looked like. On one particular summer morning, all seemed like the normal weekly event… until it wasn't. Though summer, it wasn't abnormally hot or uncomfortable, yet I could feel my anxiety (unaware at that age what anxiety was) rising rapidly. Suddenly I felt my vision begin to blur as blackness closed in on me. Gradually, as though entering a tunnel of darkness, my visibility window grew smaller and smaller until there was nothing at all but darkness.

I came to lying on the church pew with my dad under my head, and my sister fanning me off with a weekly bulletin. As the tingly blurriness began to subside I noticed myself feeling refreshed… no longer overwhelmed. Then in the next moment I became painfully aware of everyone in the surrounding pews staring down at me, no doubt concerned about this young girl who suddenly lost consciousness. I felt the blood instantly rush to my face and scrambled to get up, not wanting to draw any more attention than I already had and feeling quite embarrassed. I was wisely encouraged to stay seated and rest.

This scenario repeated itself again about a year later, though this time I knew what was coming and leaned over, signaling my Dad before I slumped onto his shoulder as the blackness took over. It wasn't until many years later through inner child work and meditation that I began to understand these occurrences more thoroughly. With the exception of the rarely held (and equally uncomfortable for me) full school assemblies, I was only in groups of that many people at church. I can clearly recall the feeling of rising anxiety that I now relate to the emotional overwhelm of absorbing the energy and feelings of those surrounding me. At that age I was not supplied with the tools I now have to understand and cope with situations such as these. A young girl in a large crowd, I could feel the energy swirling around me like a colorful whirlwind of collective emotion that threatened to take me with it. My nervous system was maxed out and unable to take any additional sensory input. Much like with overheated electronics, my system had no other choice but to shut down.

While there were parts of my spiritual upbringing that were beautiful and beneficial to my character, I mostly recall feeling confined, misunderstood, and even resentful. My highly sensitive self did not feel spiritual presence and peace dressed up in our same church pew every Sunday. I felt most spiritual and connected to a higher power and the world around me when surrounded by wildlife, basking in the colors of a vibrant sunset, or dancing around the yard, climbing trees and picking flowers, never far from an animal friend. I never understood why "God" would want us to cram into a service that was riddled with showmanship and masculine ego when the creation of God felt most celebrated (to me) when outdoors in full appreciation of it. While I loved music, the somber and traditional hymns sung out of habit instead of joy, felt as though the most important part of them was missing... soul.

No building in the world is the sole house of Spirit, nor does one particular type of service or worship govern the spiritual. Godliness, Holiness, and Spirit can be found within life itself. Spiritual living transcends the bounds of religion, for much of these lines are illusionary... created to foster separation, division, and even war, instead of unity and peace. Plenty can be learned from an open mind and the seeking of wisdom from many religions and spiritual belief systems, not just the one you happen to have grown up within. Surrendering to the energy of the Universe instead of seeking control and rigid framework of that which is, allows for the discovery of a life more aligned than you may have previously conceived.

After spending much of my early twenties struggling through a loss of identity, an abusive relationship, and bouts with anxiety and depression I finally discovered that within surrender lies peace. By honoring ourselves and our gifts we are serving our higher power and those around us in need. And by fine-tuning our empathic abilities, we are able to communicate on an energetic level that directly links us to spirit. The spirit (or soul) that exists in us can be found in other living beings of all kinds, and the existence of such does not dissipate when the breath of life leaves our body.

Some of you reading this may question whether this is truly possible, and if that is you, I understand. You have the right to doubt and question this possibility and I would much prefer that to following with blind faith. However, I am not here to convince you... I am only here to share the knowledge obtained through my own experience and of many others who have fostered the gift of spiritual communication. In order to proceed with this section of the chapter, you must be open to the possibility of more than what we are able to experience with our five senses. Since you already are aware of an ability that goes beyond these five, I hope you'll continue this journey of discovery with an open mind.

I fully believe that those who have crossed over are very present in our lives and many even seek to communicate with us regularly. I also believe we all have the capabilities to be able to tune into spirit, but empaths especially house within themselves all the necessary gifts and abilities to do so. We often talk ourselves out of it before we even begin, allowing the ego to supersede our heart-centered feelings. When we let the heart lead and connect more deeply with our own intuition, we invite loving communication from the other side.

Children are often far more perceptive of the spiritual world than we can imagine, as their veil of societal acceptance and illusions of what is "normal" has yet to obscure their view of the world. I was reminded of this recently as my two year old was playing outside. She exclaimed, "I'm playing with my sister!"

I initially dismissed this exclamation without much thought. Perhaps she got this from a movie or book in which there was a sister relationship. Then as she grew more insistant and matter-of-fact, she explained that her sister was "right here", pointing beside her. She seemed almost annoyed that I was unaware of the obvious, and insisted upon her presence beside her.

"She likes to run too, see?" She giggled and interacted with the air beside her as though a friend was playing along. I paused for a moment, reflecting upon what she'd said.

"Is your sister older than you or younger than you?" I asked, pondering about the possibility of a spiritual presence.

"She's older"

"Is she a little older or a LOT older?" I asked, halfway prompting that she was a lot older.

"Umm… she's only a little older Mommy."

I looked around her in disbelief, smiling and aching alike in remembrance. Only a few months before my daughter was conceived I had suffered a miscarriage. Though we weren't far enough along to determine the gender, I felt sure that little baby lost was a girl. I was considering the possibility that my daughters, one never held within my arms and the other physically present, were playing together with no dimensional veil between them. As I was doing so a cardinal flew to land in the tree just above them, singing joyfully with reassurance.

Have you ever seen a particular bird or butterfly that brought with it a peaceful presence of a familiar family member or friend? Have you seen a uniquely distinct sight, a name, maybe even a certain number that reminded you of a loved one who has passed and just happened to show up right when you were needing a little extra reassurance or encouragement? It's easy to pass these moments off as happenstance or allow our ego to convince us they are coincidence. But by observing them open-mindedly, meditating or praying on them, and logging your instances of connection as well as the feelings experienced, you'll begin to see patterns and connections that would have been easily brushed over had we not given the invitation for our intuition to take the lead.

Here are a few ways spiritual communication may come through:

- Animal messages

From what I've shared with you so far, it would make sense that animals would be one of the first forms of spiritual communication I'd experience. Animals are excellent messengers, as they are intuitive beings by nature (we are too, though we often allow ourselves to forget this). I've asked my spirit guides to show me a particular animal in demonstration of their guidance and they deliver. Find a resource, a website or book, that you're able to find spiritual meanings of animals and stick to that same resource. You'll be amazed at how many times the sighting of a specific animal holds a message that provides guidance and support.

- Symbols

Often we relate certain objects… foods, decor items, clothing or jewelry to a person we love who has passed or a spiritual experience. These objects allow us to connect deeply with the memories you hold together and invite your loved one to connect with relative ease. If you see an object that reminds you of someone who has passed, take a breath and allow yourself to truly feel their presence. Mentally, or out loud, invite them to provide guidance or a message they wish to share when this occurs.

- Audible messages

Sometimes you may hear a word or sentence as though spoken from a loved one or higher power. These messages may sound like a unique thought that spontaneously popped into your head with no followable train of thought that preceded them.

- Numbers

Have you ever noticed the same numbers that hold a special meaning to you pop into your life? Whether you're glancing at the clock or pass a certain license plate that catches your eye, these instances are not coincidence. The spiritual world like to remind you of their presence with this simple visual and repetition of numbers, often called "Angel Numbers" hold special meanings.

- Electronics

This mode of communication can seem quite fun for the spiritual world. Due to their energetic existence, moving objects is more of a challenge and requires significant energy output on their part. Communicating through electronics on the other hand, is far easier and requires less energy. This mode can come in the form of electronic malfunctions that either require you to stop and think about a particular message, lights turning on, off, or pulsing to remind you they are near, or a certain song with a much needed message popping on the radio at just the right time. During an intuitive reading in which I was communicating with a woman's deceased mother, the lights in the room I was in flickered intensely with every strong message I felt come through. The flickering and pulsing then receded during the times I was feeling her presence but not a message, which helped to validate her words to me and her daughter.

- Feathers or coins

These little gestures of spiritual presence remind us we are not alone and are easier physical objects to manipulate by spiritual energy. You may notice a particular coin make its appearance, or a feather show itself just as you were needing some extra guidance or support. When feathers or coins seem to "randomly" appear in your life, take note of the thoughts or feelings that come with them. These intuitive feelings or thoughts are likely exactly the message the spiritual world is intending to share with you.

- Mist, shadows, and figures

Some, typically those who have clairvoyant abilities, are able to visually see spirit. They can be frequently recognized by a soft mist or haze, a shadow in the corner of your eye, or the shape of a human figure. These appearances are often gone as quickly as they appear and can leave one questioning what they saw. If you suspect you may have seen spirit, pay attention to how you feel. I will often see a mist or hazy figure in the corner of my eye and when I turn to look fully, it disappears. However, as I do so and tune into my inner guidance I notice the thoughts and feelings that arise correlate with a particular person and often contain a message of love and support.

- Cold or gentle breeze

When experiencing a spiritual visitor, you may suddenly feel the need to put on a cozy sweater and warm socks. Spirit often brings feelings of cold and when I am feeling strong spiritual guidance from a particular individual who has passed or simply from the Universe/God, I often feel my hands and feet grow cold. You may also experience a soft breeze or wind where it may not make sense to feel one, such as somewhere in your home or a building where drafts would not be found. Perhaps when in a protected space outdoors you feel complete stillness, followed by a spontaneous little gust that gives you a burst of intuitive guidance just as sudden.

- Light

Some empaths and intuitives are able to recognize spiritual presence through flashes, twinkling, or swirling light. It is important to be cognizant of these experiences, as they can also be symptoms for medical concern. If all is well and they are not health related, enjoy these bursts of light knowing you are being visited by spirit. Personally when I'm feeling especially aligned and supported, or need a reminder of how blessed I truly am, I see twinkling lights in the upper range of my vision that appear all over and are gone within five to ten seconds. These may be white light, or you may see flashes of color that correspond to a spiritual energy or the message you're intended to receive.

- Dreams

Spiritual connection and guidance often appears where there is little resistance. Our cognitive activity during sleeping and dreaming allows for messages to come through without intervention from our ego, challenging our belief and dismissing things that may seem out of the ordinary or coincidental. Whether people, animals, or situations and environments speak to your subconscious, this is an excellent time to allow yourself to tune in during lights out. Keep your journal on your bedside table or easily within reach immediately upon waking. Dreams can quickly fade away and recede into the depths of our lost memories as we reacclimate to our waking life. Jotting down a few notes or recording audio of the guidance received may help you to connect the dots with current happenings in your life. There was a dream I had of a client of mine that seemed to not have any blatant message or connections at first. However, after casually communicating the dream contents to them, they had a look of disbelief on their face. I had just described precisely the activity (not typically a part of the schedule) that had taken place the night before and unknowingly tied it to a message of support and guidance by sharing.

However they choose to connect and you're able to perceive them, open your heart and mind to the support they have to offer! Keep your own vibrations high and centered in love to attract only loving and positive spiritual energy. If you notice yourself experiencing something new, or first becoming aware of it, demonstrate your feelings of gratitude toward the spiritual world for showing themselves to you. While the first experiences you feel may seem startling, avoid responding from a place of fear as lower vibration energy attracts lower vibration spiritual presence. Applying the principles of Part Three in this book also ensures you are calling in only the highest good to support your spiritual journey.

Connecting with your Spirit Guides

Imagine how you would feel if you knew that you could connect with a council full of wisdom, love, and support at all times? This is not simply a constructed idea... this is your reality if you choose to accept it, if you choose to do the work to connect with the spiritual world around you. I truly believe we are all given guides, guardian angels, spirit guides, wise ancestors or however your theology supports you framing it within your own mind. We are all given a tribe of support that transcends our physical realm. Imagine as you go about your day, that you have spiritual beings ready to come to your aid and provide you with messages to help guide you along your path of love. This is the path your soul has chosen, not a path riddled with fear and burdened by your ego-driven thoughts. It truly is possible.

You may have heard stories of guardian angels or people who have passed watching over someone. There are countless anecdotes of such experiences that are validated by a simple sign or occurrence that only makes sense when associated with the person that has passed. There are books and blogs dedicated to this very topic, allowing us to feel confident in the fact that death is not the end and that our spirit continues on. If our spirit does not end with the death of our physical body, wouldn't YOU choose to encourage, support, and uplift those that you love with your presence? My answer is undoubtedly yes. I love knowing that I will continue to be in the lives of my loved ones and able to guide them in special ways while looking out for their safety and well-being. We are all loved by not only those who have passed that we are aware of, but also ancestors and spiritual guides beyond what we know in our current life. I have been able to connect with guides or angels of my own, only a couple of which I was aware of in this physical lifetime, yet they continue to make their presence known and guide me along my spiritual path and soul's journey.

My initial connection with my spirit guides was a powerful experience. Listening to a guided meditation, I was prompted to mentally ascend upward within a tunnel of light. As I began to reach a deeply meditative state of consciousness. I envisioned this tunnel or cylinder of light to be a vibrant blue that connected from the earth up to a place beyond the stars in our galaxy. When I felt to be about midway up, my ascension began to slow as my own doubts and fears began overtaking my mind. Just when I feared this would be unsuccessful and and connecting with my guides the way I'd intended would elude me, I saw in my mind's eye a beautifully glowing horse spirit come down to meet me. As I flung my arm around her I smelled the comforting smell of Phoenix, my beloved horse from childhood that was my loving companion and at times, my closest confidant. She gently brought me up the rest of the way through the tunnel of light where there were a few figures making their way toward me. The first (other than Phoenix) to step forward was my Uncle Bill, who also happened to be my Godfather… the man chosen by my parents to guide and support me throughout this life on Earth. He had come through to me before, and I felt he'd he'd already taught me as much from beyond as he'd guided me while present in this physical realm. He lovingly welcomed me the way he used to talk to me when I was a young girl, his voice and words full of kindness and support. He reminded me that he continues to be my voice of reason and serves as an angelic protector. Then was Cho Chen, my healing guide that I became introduced to through Reiki with my Reiki Master friend and mentor, and had yet to connect with much beyond his assistance when providing hands-on healing sessions. He welcomed me with a deep bow of respect and I returned this gesture of honor and love.

Then, my great-grandmother stepped forward. She gently gave me permission to call her by her first name... Ruth. Though I'd known her for only my younger years until about the age of 5 or 6, I always felt connected to her deeply. From her nurturing way of being, to her artistic talents and creative soul, to her love for birds and the natural world, I've often felt there to be much we had in common. She shared that she is my creative expression guide and invited me to call on her for peace and inspiration when creating and sharing my gifts. The final guide to come forward was more subdued and quiet in her presence, and I had a more difficult time connecting with her as I could feel my deeply meditative state slowly fading. She was a Native American elder... a grandmotherly woman with wise eyes and a knowing heart. She said "Ayita" with her arms outstretched to me and while I wanted to know her name and who she was, I felt this name she spoke was in reference to me. She was my nature and earth medicine spirit guide. I longed to connect with her more deeply as my trance-like state began to fade and I became aware again of my physical surroundings.

As you could imagine, I ended this meditation feeling immensely supported and encouraged. I had a tribe of spiritual beings surrounding that invited me to call upon them as needed and overwhelmed me with such unconditional love. But I was also confused and desperately wanted to know more. Who was this Native woman and what did the name Ayita mean? Was she a part of the reason I'd had a deeply ingrained curiosity and love for Native ways of life? I could recall a book I'd devoured again and again during childhood about a young Cherokee girl. I felt a closeness with her story, as though it stirred up some repressed emotions within my soul. I wondered if I'd be able to find the name Ayita anywhere and as a quick search online allowed me to discover the meaning, and I burst into delighted laughter. "Ayita" was discovered to be a Cherokee female name that meant "first to dance", a form of movement that has been pouring out of my body since before I could walk. In case these synchronicities weren't enough… the family farm where I spent my entire childhood is located in the town of, you guessed it, Cherokee!

I set aside a little time to reconnect with her alone a few days later during meditation. Upon feeling her presence once again, I asked her the questions I'd been holding onto. She seemed bothered by my reference to her as a Native American grandmother and opened up more once I identified and honored her Cherokee heritage, confirming that she was indeed referring to me as "the first to dance". She helped me to find my center and remember that we are one with the earth. Guidance we are unable to discover when reflecting inward can be found through exploring the natural world, for as we get to know the ways of nature surrounding us we gain insight into ourselves.

Meditation Prompt: From a place of peace and love, center yourself with the earth and your higher power and begin taking deep breaths. As you feel your body slowly relax from head to toe, thank your spirit guides for their support in your life. If you've yet to meet or understand who your spirit guides are, you can envision a beautiful place among the stars where they are waiting for you. Visualise a gentle tunnel of light inviting you upward, allowing you to rise from your current location to a spiritual place. Feel yourself floating up and up, until you come to a clearing at the top of this light tunnel. Here you see the shadows of your guides in the distance, slowly walking toward you. As they come closer you begin to see them step forward, one at a time to greet you and show themselves to you. You may ask each one to show you a sign they will use in your daily life to connect with you and demonstrate their presence. Trust your intuition on this thought or image that pops into your mind and thank them for their unconditional guidance and support, even when unseen.

This may take several tries and is only one way of connecting with your spirit guides. To do so with a soothing meditation to guide you, visit my Youtube Channel video "Connecting with your Spirit Guides" Do not feel discouraged if you do not meet them right away, simply continue working to strengthen your intuitive muscles! This experience of meeting my spirit guides took years of intuitive growth and development.

CHAPTER THREE:

IDENTIFYING & GROWING YOUR STRENGTHS

As I previously mentioned, connecting with and fostering your intuitive gifts is a journey that requires an open mind and an open heart. Place yourself in a time of childhood innocence where you believed fully in magic and found beauty in the simplest of places. Reconnect with that inner child before you were told what was possible and impossible. That young child who knew their abilities and gifts without fear or judgement... they were completely right. You are capable of growing a dash of curiosity into a skill you feel confident in, or a smidgeon of familiarity and interest into a life-altering calling capable of healing your wounds and empowering others to do the same.

We are taught to seek our answers and inspiration from external sources. There is great benefit in working with mentors, reading self-growth books, and watching educational videos to better our lives. There is much to be learned from the experiences and wisdom of others. I've written this book to be held by your hands for that very reason. But allow me to ask you an important question to reflect upon.

Do you spend as much time seeking answers and inspiration from within as you do outside of yourself?

In order to fully understand and grow our strengths, we have to allow for our intuitive connection to be deepened. Think of a time when you were looking for guidance and support when making an important decision. You received a friend's opinion, read a page within a spiritual book, or perhaps sought the advice of a mentor... only to immediately agree wholeheartedly with their response with the knowledge that the choice they felt would be best was also what you felt too. Or perhaps be struck with the impulse to argue, knowing that you intuitively felt the opposite option was the right choice for you. So often we seek to receive answers to our life's purpose and guidance by looking outside of ourselves instead of choosing to connect so deeply to our inner self that our decisions cannot help but flow in aligned synchronicity.

In our current day and age we are able to seek that external support and validation so rapidly that it has become an obsession for many. Forums and reviews at our fingertips make choosing a new bike an endeavor that seems to require hours of research and surveying those you are in contact with. Even seemingly enjoyable activities such as deciding on a fresh haircut and style or planning your child's birthday party have become decisions in which online board compilations and images take over your decision-making. In belonging to a local "Mamas" group on Facebook, I was saddened to see the number of questions asked that demonstrated a severe disconnect from the power and strength of a mother's intuition. Many of these threads were overtaken by well-intentioned responders, whose contradicting answers only served to further confuse the mother who posed the original question. While pages such as these exist to connect and help one another, we can easily fall into the trap of feeling unable to make intuitive decisions without the consultation of one or many others who may seem knowledgeable on the subject. A few short decades ago we only had the ability to directly ask close family and friends for their advice and guidance, and that was where the validation ended. Now, many struggle to make decisions without the consultation of far beyond those within close proximity to our life path, many times even strangers. So what do we do about this?

We have the opportunity of working to understand and strengthen our own intuitive gifts in such a way that feelings of connectedness with our higher self or higher power reclaim their place within our minds. Instead of being plagued with doubt, uncertainty, and fear, we are able to move forward with confidence, understanding that each step along the way is supported by our magic roadmap... our intuition. This roadmap, when followed, will not lead us astray.

It is likely that you identify with one or more of the intuitive gifts mentioned in Chapter Two, and if not, that's completely okay! There is no need to feel overwhelmed by them or put pressure on yourself to explore all of these gifts at once. You are awakening to them in perfect timing and if you seek them, they will reveal themselves to you. Were there any descriptions that made you exclaim, "Yes! That's me!"? or brought you back to a particular place or event in time? These may be gifts you can recall having a tendency toward in young childhood, and have memories of these rising to the surface. Perhaps one or more resonated strongly with you and felt as though it spoke to you most. You may feel especially curious about a particular gift and feel inspired to research it further. These are the gifts and abilities to start focusing on and practicing with first. If you currently practice or experience more than one of these, sharpen them with care and allow them to lead you in opening up more doors to intuitive cohesiveness.

When seeking to grow your gifts, each and every one can be enhanced by working to strengthen and reconnect with your intuition. Intuition is the obvious root of these gifts, and the means in which information comes through to you. A common visualization tool used in meditation and energy healing is to envision yourself as a hollow bone or tube. Through this hollow bone flows the spiritual and intuitive gifts you've been given to share. These gifts are not from you, they are from a higher power, a greater source of unconditional love and light. You have the honor and responsibility to cherish, nurture, and share these gifts by allowing them to flow through you. In meditating or praying on this visualization, it helps to relieve feelings of anxiety or burden. It is not necessary to tirelessly strive toward a desired outcome, forcing yourself on at a rate that feels uncomfortable and strained. Instead, slowing down and tuning inward allows these gifts to flow. You don't need to feel it is your duty to be the source of inspiration or healing for others, just open yourself up and allow the hollowness to be filled by an infinite love. Then share that message of love in the unique ways that only you can.

Using this visualization helped me immensely in my hands-on healing practice. Before studying Reiki and receiving my attunements, I was aware there was a significant energy exchange taking place. I would finish sessions feeling particularly overwhelmed and exhausted, and it took all the effort I could muster to finish out a full day of clients. Though I was passionate about the healing work I was doing, I knew I could not continue on this way for much longer. I so desperately wanted my clients to experience deep and powerful healing that I was trying incredibly hard to make that happen. I took full responsibility as to whether they felt healing and placed much of my own self-worth within this realm of dependency. Emotionally exhausted and physically strained from working so hard to heal those on my table, I knew there had to be a better way. Through my Reiki Master's guidance, she encouraged me to let go… to surrender their healing to a higher power of good and learn to be hollow. While it took some practice to do so completely, I found my healing practice to be forever changed. I was no longer fatigued and energetically drained after every session, as the energy required for helping my clients heal was not coming from me... it was coming through me. I was not the source of the healing. My part was simply to be an unresisting conduit to the healing energy and love of the Universe.

This same concept can be applied in any realm of work or play by asking yourself, "How can I allow myself to be hollow, inviting the love of the Universe to flow through me?" Release attachment to the outcome of your intentions, having faith that if you are supported and guided in doing so the result will be too... even if not easily observable at first.

Intuition Enhancing Activities:

- Dedicate time for connecting with your intuitive voice through meditation. Allow your breath to deepen and relax as you focus on the inhale and exhale gently quieting your mind. Ask yourself, what is my intuition trying to tell me? Without judgement, allow whatever thoughts you have to arise and observe the emotional response that comes with them.

- Listen to your body. Set mental or physical alarm reminders to pause and tune in. Are you holding tension in any particular areas? Are you noticing your body signalling when you are neglecting your intuitive voice? (examples: headaches when feeling overwhelmed and unfocused, gut sensitivities when feeling nerves or lack of trust), tension in a particular part of your body that you associate with a person or situation) How can you better listen to the signals your body is giving you before they become uncomfortable or even painful?

- Journal or write out your thoughts. Ask your intuition about questions or concerns that have been plaguing you as if you're writing to ask a close friend. Then breathe deeply and allow the answers to flow through your pen or pencil without stopping to question or correct the responses.

- Take action. Allow yourself to be impulsive within reason. Don't allow your mind time to overanalyze or talk you out of the decision your intuition is strongly guiding you toward and instead act quickly.

- Take note of your "aha" moments. Often ideas, insight, and advice can come to us in a sudden way that feels completely spontaneous and unrelated to your previous train of thought. If unable to act on these right away (as they often come through when stirring at night, in the line at the grocery store, or another equally inconvenient time), jot these ideas down in a notebook.

- Play intuitive guessing games. Have an inkling that a certain person is calling before you pick up the phone to see? Suspicious that a major life event is about to happen in someone's life? Make guesses about what is occurring or will occur and watch your intuition gain strength.

CHAPTER FOUR:

ESSENTIAL EMPATH HEALING

We are at a pivotal time in the history of humankind, and YOU, my friend, are not becoming aware of your gifts by accident. You may have heard the phrase "the veil is thinning", when referring to spiritual connection and perception of things beyond what our 5 traditional senses are able to pick up. You are a part of this process, as your understanding of your own gifts and how they can help those around you is what has the capability to heal this Earth. The human inhabitants of our planet need as much help as the earthly environment around us. Have you ever seen photos of areas abandoned by humans throughout the world? Eventually the industrial structures and buildings are overtaken by wildlife of all kinds and returns the area to a natural environment, barely distinguishable from the natural world around them. We simply have to slow down our pattern of destructive behaviors, open up to the magic of healing, and allow Mother Nature to do her thing. The same process applies for human kind, simply slow down and allow the healing to take place throughout our species.

How do we do so? By positively affecting the hearts of humankind, we have the ability to heal. If the weight of this topic is feeling quite substantial, or is even anxiety-inducing, that is okay! It is simply affirming once again that you are indeed an empath. In feeling the energy of life around us, we often feel overwhelmed by the pain felt throughout the world during times of trauma or disaster. With current times and many around us only amplifying this pain and panic, it can feel even more draining to think about. Which is why I'd like to take a moment to remind you… it is not YOUR responsibility to heal the world. Repeat that one with me out loud:

It is not my responsibility to heal the world.

However… it is essential that you do the work needed to heal YOURSELF in order to help our planet heal and rise together. All you really need to do is work on yourself. The need to heal our soul reaches far past the effect of our own life. Any deep healing work that is neglected or repressed has the potential of being passed down to the next generation. By refusing to acknowledge and work on these areas that require healing, no matter how minor we consider them to be, the beliefs we hold about ourselves and others are affected. When our belief system is affected, our behavior displays this… directly impacting the way we interact with or raise the next generation. For example, a father who has internalized painful remarks and lack of support, encouragement, or love in his own own life may be likely to repeat this behavior toward the next generation. Even if this is not the case, his lack of self-confidence because of such experiences is demonstrated through his example. The way he carries himself, his internal dialogue and audible self-talk, and decision making all exemplify these unhealed areas of self. By doing the inner work discussed in the following chapters to identify patterns of harmful behaviors and limiting beliefs, you are acknowledging areas of yourself that need a little extra love and care. Then taking the initiative to apply the essential tools we discuss together in Chapters six, seven, and eight, you are able to heal and grow... opening your heart to be of greater service to those around you to be a mighty force of compassion in this world.

In doing so, you will naturally take part in a process referred to in spiritual teachings and shamanic texts as shadow work and light work. While the sound of these two areas of healing may seem to be polar opposites, they are actually deeply related. One cannot exist without the other as they are intertwined within the dance of soul healing.

Shadow work is done when we fully embrace and seek to understand the darker, traditionally more negatively viewed aspects of our life and world views. Perhaps the most important of these to look closely upon is fear. Whenever a fear is brought to the surface, the triggering of that fear is an invitation to lean in. It is our instinctive nature to feel the tendency to shy away from fear. We believe that in doing so we will avoid feeling the intensity of emotion. Avoidance of such opportunities to heal and grow will only lead to a recurrence of them until the soul lesson they've brought along with them is learned.

The emotion of fear exists to keep us safe from harm and danger, real or imagined. Unfortunately for many, the majority of these fears exist only within the illusions of our imagination. These are the fears that shadow work invites us to overcome. In order to do so, we must be willing to meet these fears where they are currently and investigate the reasons in which they exist. Healing and transformation occur when we intentionally choose to turn toward fear instead of turning away from it.

When my daughter was a few months old and I was recovering well from the long labor and emergency cesarean section that brought her into this world, I knew I needed to get back into practicing yoga more fully. I was craving for my body to feel like my own again, and knew I needed the mental and emotional peace brought to me by rolling out my mat and surrendering to familiar movement. And boy, did doing so feel gooood! At first I struggled to accept my inflexibility, and loose softness of my midsection that growing an entire human brings about... but as I continued returning to my mat I grew to appreciate my body in an entirely new light. I slowly healed and strengthened areas that needed it most and gave myself grace in doing so, celebrating all the little wins along the way. Yet there was a component of my practice that I deeply enjoyed since childhood, and had not done since midway through my pregnancy. Backbends.

Backbends, or wheel pose, is a maneuver in which you are

doing just that… bending backward until your feet and hands are all completely on the floor and abdomen in the sky creating an arch, much like an upside down "U" shape. This pose is a wonderful heart-opening stretch to relieve tension in the back, release the neck and shoulders and feel invigorated throughout your body. I'd always loved the relief this pose gave me and it would be placed toward the top of my list of favorites. However, this stretch that my body was aching for presented an entirely new fear.

I was legitimately concerned that my c-section scar would bust open. This fear involved an animated imagining of where I'd been sewn back together reopening, spilling my insides out like a toy animal sliced open with stuffing exploding from the opening. While I knew parts of this fear were illogical, I did understand that my fear originated from the very real possibility of creating immense pain in the areas that had already experienced more physical pain than I'd ever imagined being capable of withstanding. The fear itself was displayed in a way that my brain could recognize wasn't exactly realistic, but this mental imagery was providing me with an opportunity to understand where the fear was coming from. I could then move forward by choosing to do the shadow and light work needed by leaning into the fear.

Through my yoga practice and meditation I began my shadow work. I got in touch with where the fear originated… a place of deep pain and emotional darkness. I embraced this feeling of revisiting the pain, something that I had not done until that point. In doing so, I cried many tears. Ones of reliving the physical pain of a forty hour labor and of having to forgo the natural labor and delivery I had envisioned for myself, as well as the attachment that came along with that dream. Tears of missing that first snuggle and the foggy, pain-filled memories of the first week of our daughter's life. Tears of being reliant on my husband and mother to help me care for my baby as I could barely care for myself, and of painfully shuffling one foot in front of the other to make it to the bathroom only to cry out in pain and frustration. Tears of releasing the attachment to what I believed I'd lost and centering myself in remembrance of what a beautiful life I'd gained.

It was time to bring these shadows to light and face my fear. I reassured my mind and body that much healing had occurred since then, and gently massaged the point of incision with love. I encouraged myself by easing into my stretching in a similar way and with every stretch I was observing the delicious feeling of lengthening while appreciating that there was no pain or major pulling in the area. I'd come so far! I slowly eased into a gentle backbend while observing the feeling of strangeness, much like when you put jeans on for the first time in early fall after many months of wearing only shorts. It feels familiar, but somehow completely different. As you may have already suspected, my guts did not fluff out onto my yoga mat and much to my pleasure… my incision scar held. While I still felt weak and sore, unable to hold the pose for long, I knew this additional means of stretching and strengthening would be beneficial to my body, mind, and spirit. And most importantly of all, I had conquered my fear of the shadows and brought this fear to the light. In doing so I had the opportunity of inspiring other hesitant c-section mamas that they truly could return to their full practice, as long as tuning into their body and listening to the signs it gave them was top priority.

Shadow and light work are like two sides of the same coin. One cannot exist without the other. A common trend within the world of metaphysical healing and spiritual growth is a tendency to focus more on lightwork and overlook the shadows. It requires less vulnerability to paste on a smile and focus only on the light aspects than to dive deep into the challenge of the dark.

Consider the life of a seed and young plant. Before the plant emerges into the light to provide joy and sustenance to other living creatures it must spend a significant time underground in the soil. The seed must take up water from the surrounding soil, cracking open the seed coat. This process does not happen instantly and involves transformation that may seem uncomfortable at times. During this time of residing in shadows below the surface, the change that takes place is setting up this tiny plant baby for future abundance. The plant embryo reaches its root out into the surrounding soil, searching for more water. Soon after the root emerges from the seed, the stem ventures out into the darkness trusting that in navigating through the shadows it will discover the light.

Like the seed, once you've embraced your experience within the soil and begin to emerge into the sunlight, you are ready for your light work. Light work is the process of taking what you've discovered through your shadow work and using it to illuminate your own life and the lives of others. Some of you may feel called to share the intricate details of your own journey, understanding that there will be many who resonate with the lessons you've learned. You may find yourself called to do so through conversation, writing, speaking, or whatever form of creative expression you choose. Regardless of whether you decide to share or not, the act of internalizing the lessons learned in order to respond to others with compassion instead of reacting out of fear lights the way for other people to rise. You are capable of healing others simply by completing the light and shadow work it takes to heal your own soul.

Journaling prompt: What fears or areas of shadow are keeping me from living life to the fullest of my ability? In what ways can I lean into these fears and recognise their potential for healing and growth? How might my life (and the lives of those around me) be different if I am able to bring these shadows to the light?

CHAPTER FIVE:

HEALING THE
DEPTHS WITHIN

Somewhere along your journey as an empath your ego chose to see your sensitivity as a weakness… as something that makes you "less than". You may have been told to "toughen up" or "stop being so sensitive", which planted the idea in your head. We've nurtured this idea subconsciously by allowing it to resurface any time you felt insecure or fearful, when there was a time that you noticed your sensitivity making you feel different from those around you. Imagine if instead, you're able to recognize this ego-driven response as the natural response you've conditioned yourself to display. Imagine if instead you took note as though an outside observer of this response instead of allowing an insecurity or fear to fuel the misguided illusion that your empath ability or sensitivity is something that makes you weaker than those around you. What if instead you were able to recognize when that tendency surfaced, observe and simply let it go? Replace that ego-conceived story and instead accept the loving response that this is my beautiful gift… this is my superpower.

Like many empaths, I've chosen experiences throughout my life that have led to trauma and pain. It is my deeply ingrained belief that while those situations are unfortunate and painful, we chose our soul's journey within this body for a reason. I know you may be reflecting on this thought while mentally exclaiming… "Chose?! You think I WANTED to put myself through this painful experience?!". I understand this frame of thinking, as I was there not long ago myself.

In my late teens into my early twenties I was in a relationship that had me head over heels. I was enamored with this young man, and the beginning of our relationship was filled with such romantic displays of affection and love that I was hooked. This was the stuff fairytales were made of, and life outside of our relationship ceased to exist. As with many unhealthy relationships, it began like a whirlwind. I was an insecure young woman who'd been taught to rely on others to make decisions, and I felt he understood me. He understood my sensitivity and knew how to make me feel special. My family had their suspicions of him, and my mother expressed her concerns… yet I felt she had concerns over any guy I had interest in, so I didn't take them seriously. After all, the majority of our time together did not involve others and was a life within our own little world of idealistic illusion. I was romanced with experiences straight out of a movie, which played directly into my ego-centered idea of how a relationship should be.

You see, he was an energy vampire who understood my gifts and abilities, using them to manipulate my feelings at will. And I, being the empath who had yet to understand what being an empath meant, was a malleable creature... hungry for acceptance and people-pleasing to the detriment of my character. Codependency ran amuck as neither of us seemed to be able to stand on our own two feet or know who we were without the other. I did not understand that without setting your own boundaries, they will be set by others. It took months after finally leaving the relationship to fully understand the depth of emotional and sexual abuse that took place.

Upon leaving that relationship I would have loved to look back and say I found myself again and immediately felt free but that is not how my story went. Living alone in a new city, I was plagued with anxiety. Stories planted by the emotional abuse and watered by fear grew to take over my life. I was constantly on guard in my home, afraid he would show up unexpectedly or do something to sabotage my life, something I knew he was fully capable of... because he threatened to do just that. My anxiety disorder grew as I allowed my mind to continue cycling around the stories of fear. It felt as though a dark wave overtook me, and I was not in control of my life or what was happening in it.

Without the emotional understanding that I needed to stand up in knowing of my truth, my rights, my boundaries... I allowed my life to be dictated for me. If you had told me years ago that I had chosen this experience, I would have argued, likely cried, and dismissed your theories. I surely didn't intend to get myself into a relationship that required filing a police report and fearing he would show up at my door or in my home uninvited. I didn't ask for years of working through anxiety disorder and intense post-traumatic, stress induced panic attacks.

After navigating through this experience and several years on the other side I was aware that while I'd healed enough to move forward, there was something raw that remained. It surfaced when I'd face an unexpected trigger and, regardless of the public or private setting, I was reduced to a hyperventilating mess. I clearly had some deep healing left to do. I'd put an ego sized bandage over the splinter of my experience, hoping to bypass the painful work of digging it out and cleansing the wound.

During my time of denial and convincing myself I was doing great, I met a woman (the timing of which, nothing less than divine) that sparked my curiosity. She talked of things I'd yet to know and somehow they felt strangely familiar. I would bombard her with questions whenever I had the chance. As my life slowly opened to new possibilities... those of immense hope and joy, my friendship with her grew.

Shimen was a healer, full of spiritual wisdom with a heart wide open to animals and people in need of healing. She understood the healing powers of the Universe itself... ways of holistic energy healing that dated back centuries and taught me of worlds unknown. One day I boldly, seeming to have lost my social filter, asked her if she would be my mentor of sorts. She smiled, perhaps a combination of pleasure and puzzlement, and asked what I thought that meant. I admitted that I had know idea, I just felt that I was supposed to ask her that particular question.

Not long after my understanding that I had much to learn from Shimen, I finally allowed my brimming curiosity and intuition to take the lead and scheduled my first Reiki and Crystal Healing session with her. Still slightly skeptical but trusting in her, I looked online to see if I could obtain the basic understanding of what this even meant. Despite my underlying feeling of familiarity, I'd never experienced energy healing. I'd studied for four years for my Health Sciences degree, yet I was new to many alternative healing modalities that were bypassed for strictly modern, Western ways of thinking.

She excused the chaos of crystals and animal hair, none of which bothered me, as she chuckled about the habits of her many furry family members. I felt at home with the animals and was entranced by the many incredible crystals that seemed to be of every size, shape, and color. I was invited to lay back on her treatment table and close my eyes as the relaxing meditation music floated through the room. Shimen gently placed crystals all over my body and encouraged me to take deep, cleansing breaths. Her warm and comforting hands began calming my nervous system immediately. As she worked her way down my body in what I would eventually learn to be traditional Reiki hand placements, I felt myself drift into a dreamlike state, though I was fully aware of every moment. I felt as though I was floating outside of my body and saw vibrant colors, feeling the presence of angelic spirits all around me. My brain started to slow its hyper-active processing. I began to feel the most painful moments of the abuse arise within me, as though the splinter was slowly and steadily being drawn out. She softly said, "Ashley, you have to forgive." I felt the deep need for doing so welling up alongside the tears leaking out of the corners of my closed eyelids. "I forgive you," I felt with my entire heart, picturing his face and feeling a shift begin within myself.

You know how in the game of Jenga, with its stacked wooden blocks, there is often a wobble before the turn in which the entire tower comes crumbling to the ground? That was my wobble, and I could feel my heart soften and my tower begin to sway. Then she said with a soft knowing, "You have to forgive yourself." As I truly, deeply, and intentionally did so, I felt the physical remnants of pain from that experience that were buried deep within my body rise to the surface from what felt like the lower core of my body (no doubt my sacral and root chakras). In my mind's eye I saw a white butterfly carry the remnants of my pain out the window as my energy field could sense Shimen's cleansing above my physical body. I gasped with a sense of relief and peace as tears now flooded down my face in abundance.

My tower had fallen. What I believed to be holding against him; the frustration, hurt, and fear were not affecting me nearly as deeply as my inability to forgive myself. I needed to forgive myself for the pain I'd held onto with a death grip. For the fact that I was still in disbelief that I, a smart and talented young woman, could get myself into a mess like that. That it took me so long after the relationship ended to even admit to myself that I'd been raped and severely emotionally manipulated, simply because I didn't think that was what abuse looked like and didn't want to believe it was so. That I'd allowed my inner self to get so lost that I could hardly recognize her. I needed to forgive myself with the understanding that my highly sensitive, compassionate, and trusting heart was not to blame... that this very part of myself was exactly what I needed to reconnect with in order to heal.

This was a tower worth rebuilding. I was worth rebuilding.

It was through this experience that I began to understand how to heal and that I was truly capable of doing so. I grew to understand that the pain I had experienced was for a deeply important purpose, one I was meant to share. My intuitive gifts (once I finally chose to foster them) were far stronger and my already high levels of empathy had grown even more.

I am not the only empath who has experienced bouts of anxiety or depression. In a chaotic world of emotional bombardment, it is no wonder that many empaths suffer with anxiety and depression disorders, or a number of other mental health diagnoses such as bipolar disorder or ADHD. Navigating the complexities of your own emotions can be challenging, but combining that of one's own with the energies and emotions of those surrounding you can be overwhelming, especially before acquiring the knowledge and understanding needed to discern what is yours and what is not. Many cases of debilitating anxiety, my own for example, are a product of repressed trauma, in need of deep spiritual healing combined with emotional and energetic overwhelm and topped with sub-par self care.

Keep in mind, I share this not for use as an excuse to remain in a current state of struggle, but to remind you that you are not alone and empower you to rise above! The more we can focus on connecting with our intuition and what it is trying to tell us, the better we will be able to transcend the murky waters of anxiety, depression, and more. When these experiences arise they are a sign from our internal emotional navigation that something is not right. Perhaps your anxiety is trying to show you that your current living situation is not good for your soul, or you are working in a job that does not help you fulfill your life's purpose. Maybe your depression is trying to get your attention to work through childhood trauma, emotional abuse, or deeply ingrained insecurities. Perhaps your ADHD diagnosis is your nervous system reacting to the over-stimulation of the energies around you that you have the gift of perceiving so strongly.

Our society is finally beginning to shift and there is much more support surrounding mental and emotional health matters than ever before. While this is the case, there is still little understanding of energetic health, soul healing, and the unique predispositions and tendencies of highly intuitive beings. It is our job to seek understanding... not only from outside resources such as this book but more importantly, from within. There are times Western medicine and the prescription of pharmaceuticals is validated, and can help to balance hormones necessary for treating mental health concerns. In many cases, other avenues of healing have the opportunity of naturally completing this same rebalancing without drastically disturbing our energetic environment… though writing a prescription for 20 minutes of deep breathing or removing processed foods and high sugar content from one's diet may not be well received in many medical communities. We are often given many signs our mind, body, and soul are not in unity before it manifests into a mental or physical illness. Likewise, we have many natural pathways to follow before resorting to further medical intervention.

When pregnant with my daughter, I was still suffering from severe anxiety. Though I was unaware of the severity at the time, I knew I was struggling. I was convinced I was not going to receive the support I needed from my husband and feared our marriage was nearing the end. While I physically prepared for childbirth and read encouraging books on natural birth, I was ignoring my spiritual and mental wellness and did not understand the increased importance of connecting deeply with my intuition. I chose to receive care from a local group of midwives and began my prenatal appointments. After my first couple of appointments I brought up that I'd been really struggling with my anxiety levels and wondered if there were any recommendations they had for helping with this. Immediately the response was, "Well, we could put you on Drug X or Drug Y, both of which are safe for baby though Drug X typically has a lower risk of side effects."

There was no discussion as to my daily habits, education on natural ways to manage anxiety, or attempt to understand why the anxiety disorder was occurring. Unfortunately, this is not a unique case. Often in the world of empaths and highly sensitive beings, physical and mental health concerns are deep manifestations of unhealed trauma and pain. For example, my severe and debilitating anxiety was the product of repressed sexual and emotional abuse, root and sacral chakras in need of healing and aligning, fear and lack of emotional connection at that time within my marriage, and the disconnect I was experiencing from my spiritual and intuitive gifts. Had I been prompted to consider the root of this anxiety disorder instead of focusing on how to eradicate the terrifying symptoms, perhaps the true holistic healing could have been gently initiated.

This mentality goes far beyond my personal story. We have a societal challenge to overcome, as many have been taught from a young age that in order to feel better there is no change that must occur other than to simply "take something". Have you noticed at the mention of a headache, upset stomach, or sore joints a loving friend or family member frequently asks, "Did you take something for that?". They may even follow this question with an offer to share the pill that works best for them.

We can mask the symptoms and temporarily relieve physical pain or even numb the mental or emotional pain, but these "solutions" are only postponing the most challenging part of feeling better… the deep soul healing that is required to life your life well in mind, body, and spirit. Covering a wound with a band-aid without removing the splinter may allow it to heal over. Even after the area has appeared to heal completely, pressure in a particular spot or at a specific angle can cause it to hurt as much as when it first caused pain. And so, we must do the challenging work of uncovering the wound… becoming aware of why it is there in the first place, and removing the splinter. This experience can be almost as painful as the original but only by doing so are we offering ourselves the opportunity to truly heal and move forward with joy and ease. Focusing on the soul wounds as higher priority and the rest of our physical manifestations as secondary endeavors will allow for a shift that awakens the masses.

There are innumerable commercials, billboards, magazines, books, and digital ads dedicated to physical health and wellness. The perception that by working to be in peak physical fitness you gain overall wellness is false. Think of the most beautiful and luscious green houseplant you've come across, perhaps within your own home. We can trim the leaves that appear to be wilting or unhealthy and maintain the portion of the houseplant that resides above the soil, but if the foundational root system is unhealthy the rest of the plant will continue to suffer. By shifting our focus to begin the foundation of our wellness pyramid with heart-centered spiritual wellness instead of physical, we can heal the areas of our life that are most deeply affecting us.

But why, you may wonder, should we allow spirit to become the base of our wellness when who we are is made up of body, mind, AND spirit? If we look upon our existence as a unified triad of these three components, shouldn't they all receive equal care and attention? If focused on solely this human life experience, then yes... that would seem logical. But as we've uncovered and the vast majority of religions and spiritual belief systems teach, the spirit transcends the life of the body and existence of the mind. It is the spirit that lives on, and it is the spirit that should take priority when it comes to true healing and growth. Even the gravely ill can feel peace despite immense physical pain if their soul is content with the understanding that this is not their permanent state.

Just as there is disagreement surrounding the best way to care for the physical or mental, there is an everlasting debate as to how to properly achieve spiritual growth and enlightenment. This very disagreement among men and women has led to many wars and unbelievable destruction for centuries that still continues today. If we are to open our minds and hearts to love one another, serve one another, and become a mighty force of compassion... we must be willing to set aside our preconceived notions of the right and wrong ways to get there, for that is not up to us. To believe that the way of one religion, the way of one cultural belief system is the only way to achieve a sense of true unity is to insert our own ego into the equation.

Ego is responsible for the "my way is the best/only way" mentality, and must be quieted in order to learn from those whose spiritual background differs from your own. Unfortunately this mentality is not uncommon and can be found in almost every corner of the world. Again, the source of this lack of unity returns to fear. Evolutionarily, we seek comfort in the company of those with similar backgrounds and belief systems and fear those that differ. Back in early human history, this made far more sense as one did not know whether a tribe of humans that differed from them would make an attempt to harm or kill them. While we are evolving into a higher consciousness and more unified state of being, we must actively work to overcome our evolutionary habits. While it is understandable to be skeptical of one that differs from all you've been taught, how else are we expected to expand our horizons beyond that which has been passed down through our own lineage and close peer group? These traditions and ancestral reminders of faith or spirituality are beautiful and have much to teach us. As do the teachings of those whose belief systems differ from our own.

You see, they are not required to be in competition. Instead, different religions and spiritual beliefs throughout the world have the potential to spark new growth within your own personal journey of spirituality and healing. When we hear parables and stories told from a differing point of view, we have an opportunity to set aside our differences and listen or read from a place of love. If we do so, we will find that we have more in common within our souls than different. Which truly is the key after all, isn't it? There are beautiful souls of all faith backgrounds that are highly empathic and more inspired by bringing unity to their community than defending their status as the only way. As you navigate along your path of growth and healing, the "how" recedes and the "what" takes precedence...

...and the "what" is love.

However you're seeking to transcend your fears and pain, you must be willing to allow them to be gently quieted and replaced by love, acceptance, and forgiveness. The world we observe and create externally is a mirror to our internal peace or lack thereof. Regardless of the particulars of what you are working through, it is important to remember that your sensitivity does not make you weaker than those around you. Your ability to feel things deeply does not lessen your strength. Instead allow them to go hand in hand and allow your strength and sensitivity to merge as one. Allow yourself to sing your song, amplifying your message of love and light to those around you. We all have our traumas, our suffering and burdens. The level of which is not as important as the fact that we all know how it feels to hurt. Only some of us allow this pain to be a lesson that we learn from. When we experience something traumatic such as the unexpected death of a close loved one, abuse or neglect, even violence, we are faced with two choices. The first option is, to be blunt, the easier and more often taken path. You can choose to dwell in a place of pain and victimhood, using your experience as the excuse to remain in a place of lower vibrations. You can continue to fear those around you, expecting the same or similar experience to repeat itself and therefore manifesting more negativity into your life. You can stay here, in the safety of the familiar... or you can choose to rise. Just as the phoenix rises from the ashes, the second path provides you with an incredible opportunity to help others heal in a way that nobody else can... simply because you understand the deep and debilitating pain you've been through that they may currently be experiencing. This option is by far the most challenging to begin with, but will lead to a life full of purpose and inspiration.

Within any area of significant growth and change, fear is invited by our ego to come along for the ride. Vibrationally, few emotions resonate at a lower level than fear itself. Fear is the emotion behind wars and division among people and animals alike, causing our survival instincts to take over our rational thought and emotional organization process. Where there is fear, there is no room for love, compassion, or empathy.

When uncentered and lacking peacefulness, our brains like to play the "what if" game. What if I share this and my family disapproves? What if I put myself out there and those I respect dismiss my ideas? What if this relationship goes south? What if I try to make this business venture work and I fail? While we are hard-wired to care about what (and how) others think and feel, we must allow the love of what we do and who we are to transcend the limiting beliefs we tether ourselves to. Caring about the opinions and concerns of those closest to us keeps us grounded. Just as a stake in the ground keeps a colorful hot air balloon connected through ropes to the Earth below, we are able to feel centered and stable by the reliable support of those who care for us. However, those who love us are often concerned about keeping us safe and out of harm's way. While a hot air balloon that is tethered securely to the ground may be safe from flying away or coming across anything that may puncture its vulnerable exterior, it also never flies. A grounded hot air balloon does not have the opportunity to uplift others or bring smiles to faces far and wide with its vibrant colors and unique patterns.

We don't need to feel as though we must reach our highest heights immediately. This is a journey with ebbs and flows… a dance of rapid growth and healing, and periods of slow progress and steady release of old habits and mindset. Each step we take forward in listening to our own intuition enables us to build upon the previous and raises us higher.

In my late teens and early twenties, my decisions were made based upon what other people thought. I'd have a glimmer of intuitive inspiration only to have it recede, making way for my parent's beliefs in what direction I should be taking or allowing fear of criticism by my peers to bring me back down to the ground. When deciding what career path to choose, I was drawn to everything artistic and healing.

I pursued my Health Sciences degree while feeling lit up by my elective dance classes and inspired by the community service work. Even though I had a knowing that I was within the right realm, I was yet to feel understood and inspired. Upon graduating and sifting through hundreds of job listings,

I still felt as though I was trying to hammer a square peg into a round hole. While I could perhaps imagine myself at many of these jobs, it seems I would need to bend and compress my true self and calling in order to fit the molds these careers entailed. What was all that schooling, the intensity of finals, and challenges that came along with it for if I still didn't know what I wanted to do? I sent out applications, popped into places that caught my eye, and felt completely disheartened. I wanted to help people heal. I wanted to inspire them and help them understand that they can feel better. That they don't have to settle for... well... exactly what I was about to settle for.

I broke down feeling worthless and anxious, afraid I would not find the path I was meant for and end up someone whose life appeared to be sucked out of them by the job they forced themselves to attend every day. I curled up in a ball on my bed and with the last of my energy I asked the Universe, God, and all that is for help. "I don't know where to go from here and feel hopeless. Please help me discover my path."

I awoke with two words in my brain. Massage Therapy. It felt as though they came from outside of myself. I instantly grabbed my phone, pulling up a search to see if there were any local schools offering classes and training to become a Licensed Massage Therapist. There were two, one of which was not in an active enrolling period. I called the other, and the friendly career counselor who answered the phone excitedly shared that there was a new session beginning in only a week! I could tour immediately if I was interested, which I did and felt pulled as though by a magnetic force to do so.

Why hadn't I considered this path before? Oh wait... actually I had. I recalled a list made in my junior or senior year of high school. On it were ten potential careers in which I could picture myself and massage therapy one of them. This idea was pushed aside due to its unpredictable demand and likelihood of being a service pushed aside upon economic downturn. Nevertheless here I was, feeling a full-body yes that this was where I was meant to be at this moment in time.

Then the ego jumped in on the decision. "You just went through a four year bachelors degree program and now you're going to 'backtrack' to a career that takes less than a year to receive schooling for? You think your family, or anybody for that matter, is going to take you seriously? You just finished paying for schooling and now you're going to accumulate more debt on a spontaneous whim?" I slowly eased my ego into silence, convincing it that I would differentiate myself from the "spa massage" experience and provide massage strictly for health care purposes. I already had in depth knowledge of anatomy and physiology, and I would make certain they are aware of that. No froof, hippie music, or crystals for me, I'd maintain a path that was well-respected within the health field.

Little did I know this small step forward would gain traction toward a purpose I was yet to understand. This following of my intuition was just one small movement toward the direction in which I was intended. After graduating and starting my own business, maintaining the ego-centered belief that I was a serious, clinical massage therapist I became aware that healing is far from linear... and most certainly not only physical. And so began the journey that led me to writing this very chapter, one of soul healing and emotional awareness. One of understanding the true reason I was naturally good at massage therapy, my empathic nature and abilities, and that I was here to help people heal far more than a sore muscle.

It takes gumption to allow your truest light to shine, knowing that some may be dismissive or even in disbelief about the gifts you hold closest to your heart. However, as soon as you do you'll notice those who feel that way slowly fade to the background of your life... and others step forward. People who have similar gifts or those who are attracted to and encouraged by your light begin to gravitate to you. As you raise your own vibration and set intentions for how you envision your life to be, you call people into your journey that will more naturally support your purpose and cheer with authentic excitement as that hot air balloon of your life rises to new heights.

ESSENTIAL TOOLS FOR BECOMING A MIGHTY FORCE OF COMPASSION

CHAPTER SIX:

M: MEDITATION
& MOVEMENT

Meditation

Of the six essential tools to adopt in order to better your life as an empath, daily meditation is one of the most deeply impactful. I'll openly admit to you, committing myself to doing so was one of the hardest habits for me to adopt and practice regularly, and also one that has changed my life in an incredibly powerful way. If meditation seems intimidating to you, I understand. There was once an illusion held within my mind of zen monks on a peaceful mountain top, in an open mental space of complete serenity. I felt that if I were unable to obtain the same feeling conjured up in my mind, I was doing something wrong. If my mind were still processing the events of the day or bringing up feelings held within, the belief was held that this wasn't meditation, and I must be doing something incorrectly.

In a society that values noise, sells us devices for constant connection, and honors the title "busy", I struggled with silence. From the time I was first living on my own, I felt the need for continuous stimulation. It made me feel better to have something on all of the time. I'd have a show playing as I folded laundry or made dinner and played happy music while I bathed or drove. Time alone with my thoughts was avoided at all costs as I packed my days outside of classes and my work schedule with social gatherings and events. After years of doing so, finally the question was considered... why did I feel such a strong inclination to do so?

If I was never alone with my own thoughts I didn't have to feel so deeply. The overwhelming emotions of the extreme highs and lows that came along with being a highly intuitive empathic individual who didn't fully understand her gifts was simply TOO MUCH. By distracting myself with the storylines of predictable shows, music, or continuous communication with friends and family, I was handling the overwhelm of emotion the only way I knew how. Connecting with my inner self at the time was a confusing endeavor as I repressed the emotions I did not yet have the tools to understand and work through.

The voice of our mind is hard to quiet and is sometimes even confused with our inner self or intuition. As Michael Singer wisely said in his book, The Untethered Soul, "There is nothing more important to true growth than realizing you are not the voice of the mind- you are the one who hears it." Let's repeat that one out loud, perhaps jot it down a few times in your journal, and really let it soak in.

"You are not the voice of the mind- you are the one who hears it."

By practicing regular mindful stillness you train yourself to separate from the noise... the noise around you and the noise within you distracting from your connection with your higher self, who is completely in tune with your inner empath. Many (like my younger self) have preconceived notions of what meditation looks like and how to do so successfully. While calming instrumental music and candles or incense may be helpful, they are most certainly not required. All you need is a peaceful environment, a small amount of time, and dedication. As a busy mom, I've personally come to relish my meditation time in the peace and quiet of the early morning. Though building this habit takes consistent effort, once you've established it within your schedule it is hard to turn back. I've found myself feeling more rested, centered, and ready for the day than if I'd slept the extra hour I "sacrificed" for meditation, gentle yoga, herbal tea and journaling.

Often, as empaths, it is not our physical bodies that are too tired. Our minds are exhausted from continuously working to process the bombardment of information we are receiving not only from ourselves, but from everyone around us. Allowing our body to be still provides it with time to complete the necessary rest and repair cycle, but quieting our mind allows us to heal on a deep level. By softening our mind we are able to gently observe the thoughts and emotions that rise to the surface, inquiring within (without judgement) the reason for their presence. If we never take the time to sit with our emotions and truly allow ourselves time to feel them, we are unable to take the next step to identifiy or heal the root cause of them. Awareness of the subconscious repetitive patterns cycling around in our minds must rise in order for us to shift our mental narrative.

Many limiting beliefs that we tell ourselves regularly are habits so ingrained within us that we are completely unaware of their existence. Instead we stumble through the same cycle of problems that feels a bit like deja vu as our mental hardwiring is reinforced with every replay. Think of a limiting belief you feel about yourself, and take time during meditation to trace it back to its origin. Often if we are able to identify where we first began telling ourselves this narrative, we can recognize how unimportant it truly is and how much we have been allowing it to impact our life.

I am bad at math and don't like numbers. This is a storyline I'd been telling myself ever since I could remember... one that I believed to my very core. Despite testing into the advanced math placement in high school (and then admittedly relying on the help of a compassionate classmate), and surviving college calculus, if anyone asked what topic or subject I felt I was horrible at... my answer was math.

I therefore believed I was not good at anything that had to do with math. Even as a massage therapist independently running my own business and managing the finances and bookwork by myself, I was still convinced. Though I did it, I was still fearful of my finances and terrified come tax season that I missed something or made a detrimental mistake. Why was this? Why was I so convinced I was bad at math, despite many checkpoints along the way that logically proved otherwise?

I traced this narrative backwards through time. Before suffering through college calculus and high school math. Before the anxiety-inducing middle and elementary school timed worksheets in which we completed as many addition, subtraction, multiplication, and division problems as we could before the one minute buzzer rang. While this memory made my palms sweat and likely didn't help the situation, but I could feel that it wasn't the source. So backward even further I went, allowing my intuition and connection with my inner child to take the lead. I saw myself in the old blue-green Windstar Van riding with my parents, older sister, and older brother. My dad was shelling out practical word problems, an activity he enjoyed doing to invoke our minds during our family drives… and likely to keep these minds of ours too busy to argue or complain about the oldies music playing on the radio. Questions such as, "If I have twelve acres of corn that yields one hundred and seventy-five bushels an acre, and corn is two dollars and fifty cents a bushel, how much would this corn earn me?

My sister is seven years older than I, and my brother is four. While this question game was primarily for them, I could tell I was supposed to pay attention and learn from them as well. Every once in a while he would throw an "easier" one in the mix and I would immediately freeze up. He'd kindly tell my siblings not to answer, giving me the first chance to do so and feeling their anticipation and readiness to answer made me feel even more pressure. I grew to despise these problem-solving sessions, and made it clear that I'd rather read, listen to music, or just gaze out the window… anything was better than those darn math problems.

This experience was not deeply traumatic. My dad was well-intended and using this road trip time wisely, likely helping my older siblings to grow their math and reasoning skills. There were no ill-intended happenings or anything out of the ordinary, yet this experience began to shape a limiting belief in my own sensitive little self. Surely if I could not answer even the easier questions with the ease of which my siblings had solved the harder ones, I had to be bad at math.

Uncovering these (often completely untrue) beliefs we hold about ourselves about our mental capacities, relationship capabilities, physical appearance, and beyond requires quiet internal reflection. We must ask ourselves to travel back in time to places that are often uncomfortable, sometimes even deeply painful. We must search for and find the initial seed that planted this belief, uproot it, and make intentional effort to replace it with the kind of thought we decide to grow. One that is positive, loving, and encouraging. Replacing these limiting beliefs with positive ones allows us the opportunity to rewire our brain to create our new reality. Our physical world is only a representation of the beliefs we hold to be true, so why not create the most beautiful life we can imagine built with the love and support we would readily give a dear friend or family member?

Meditation not only gives us the opportunity to heal and reshape our mindset, it also allows us the opportunity to quiet enough to listen to that voice we've been talking about… our intuition, connection with your higher power, and energy of the Universe. While we may get intuitive hits and moments of clarity during the business of our daily life, we are more likely to experience a deeper connection with this internal compass if we set aside the time to develop a relationship with it.

Mindful stillness looks different for everybody, so take initiative to figure out what works best for you. And remember, this could easily evolve and change as you do throughout your journey. Perhaps lying on your yoga mat in savasana at the end of a yoga class is your place of mindful stillness. Maybe arriving early to your favorite park, church or place of worship to pray, soaking in a bath filled with essential oils, holding your kiddo or a loved one in comfortable silence, or even spending an extra 10 minutes in a quiet car after work before rejoining the family chaos. Just find something that works for you and develop a daily habit of it.

A Zen Proverb that serves to remind us, "You should sit in meditation for twenty minutes every day – unless you're too busy; then you should sit for an hour."

Movement

Life and energy are constantly in motion. The world around us is always moving to a rhythmic pulse, inspiring us to do the same. By thoroughly enjoying a form of movement regularly in your life, you're keeping your own energetic body from becoming stagnant. Have you ever noticed that a quick walk or dance break to uplifting music can take you from feeling mentally "stuck" to inspired and rejuvenated in only a few short minutes?

We all know that regularly moving our bodies as thoroughly as we are able is crucial for our physical health, but have you considered the effect of movement on our mental, emotional, and energetic states of being? Mentally, moving our bodies increases fresh oxygen and blood flow to the brain, relieving us of that dreaded "brain fog" and increasing our ability to focus. Emotionally we experience higher release of "happy hormones" and endorphins… allowing us to feel more content and experience lower levels of anxiety and depression. Energetically, we align our chakras (energy centers) and rid ourselves of stagnant energy which leaves us feeling stuck and uninspired.

So how do you apply this important "M" to your Empath wellness in order to be a Mighty Force of Compassion in this world? While you may already have an exercise regime, ask yourself whether this is something you enjoy or a way to keep yourself "in shape" or burn calories. Those things are important, but movement inspired by emotion and intuition is even more so. Through my hands-on healing work I've been made aware of something that is plaguing our population… a state of disconnect from our bodies. We, as a society, are in such a rush to accomplish and acquire that we've been trained to ignore the subtle signs that our bodies are trying to tell us.

Some of us learned at a young age to silence the voice that pertains to our bodies when told to toughen up or had our concerns dismissed. I once had a client who upon walking in the door I was able to assess an area of muscle tightness that was likely causing pain or discomfort. I asked her if she noticed this area causing her any problems and she responded that it had not. Once I palpated the area however, she nearly jumped off of the massage table! She exclaimed that she did not realize that area was so sore until I touched it, but it sure was.

Many of us are functioning in a severe state of disconnect from our bodies. We eat during the societally chosen meal times, instead of allowing ourselves to be guided by intuition and stopping when no longer hungry. We continue the same repetitive tasks without addressing or working to contradict the toll it has on our physical health. We ignore the early signals of pain and disease in order to keep pushing through our daily lives. The delightful thing about this separation of the body from our mind and spirit is that it's never too late to reconnect them.

Finding a form of movement that unites these three components of self supports the flow and growth of your intuition aligns you energetically. For this movement to be most effectively moving you toward a healthier life, it must be approached from a place of love and joy, not fear or hatred. Moving your body through a fitness class while mentally criticizing yourself or pushing yourself to extreme limits because you despise that one part of your body that you've decided doesn't appear as you'd like it to... this is not the kind of movement I'm talking about here.

If you already have found a form of movement that you are uplifted by, or feel intrigued enough that you believe you COULD enjoy... practice it! Work it into your daily routine for 30 days (holding space for a few days to give yourself grace). By developing a habit of practicing movement that you love and allowing yourself to be fully engulfed in it, you are also holding space for intuitive and spiritual growth.

If you're someone that is pondering and grasping for ideas... pause. Take a moment to remember when you've felt most at home in your body, where your mind and spirit were fully integrated within your body and the 3 were together as one whole. Reminisce on your childhood. Did you enjoy running through nature trails with a family member? Biking to the park with a neighborhood friend? Were you always climbing trees, playgrounds, even within your house? Look for a moment you felt complete freedom in your body to be your truest self and rekindle it! Loved running, or simply walking? Sign up for a local 5k run/walk for a cause you feel inspired to support or create a walking or jogging group of friends. Enjoyed dance lessons as a kid? Set aside thirty minutes first thing in the morning to dance your heart out to whatever music rings true to you. Express what you're feeling inside by propelling it through your body movements, letting go of negativity (your own or otherwise) with every deep exhale and every bead of sweat. If you are still trying to come up with a form of movement to adopt as your practice, or feel like your current method isn't working for you... try yoga.

Yoga is the practice of uniting the body, mind, and spirit through eight philosophical ways of thinking, also known as the eight limbs of yoga. While we often think of physical postures on a yoga mat, true yogic practice is a pursuit that continues long after your feet leave the mat. I cannot tell you how many clients I've directed toward taking up regular yoga practice for physical relief, but also for mental and spiritual peace. While living, our body houses our soul, how we care for it impacts more than just our physical health and well-being. Honoring your body by finding a form of movement that inspires you is just as important for your mental, emotional, and spiritual health as it is for your physical health.

Journal prompt: What form of movement sparks a light of happiness within your heart to imagine yourself doing? How can you incorporate more forms of movement like this within your daily life?

CHAPTER SEVEN:

FUEL & FRESH AIR

Fuel

We are energetic beings. How we receive our energy and what fuels our cells is then transmuted into the energy we output into the world. If we are fueling our body with junk, we don't operate at our fullest potential. The most important (and often overlooked) component of fueling our body mindfully is hydration. We all know this already, and yet it can be a challenge to put into practice. We are made up of mostly water, if we aren't drinking enough pure water our cells aren't able to function well. We feel foggy, our brain function and focus slows, and our body becomes inflamed. Toxins are unable to be flushed through our lymphatic system and out of our bodies.

From personal experience, starting my day with hot/warm water with lemon, either fresh fruit or a single drop of lemon essential oil, has been life-changing. Think of what a simple change that is! Before you put anything else into your body, drink a full glass of water. It jump-starts your digestive system, cleanses your body of toxins, reduces inflammation, and hydrates your cells. Have the goal in drinking half your body weight in ounces every day and more if you are pregnant, working to lose weight, or have a compromised immune system.

Food is another crucial way to provide ourselves with sustenance that can make all the difference in our mental, physical, and emotional health. Allowing yourself the freedom to support your body through dietary choices can powerfully impact your energetic health. Tuning into your body's physical responses, your mental alertness, and emotional stability following the consumption of different foods can be powerfully impactful. Notice what foods leave you feeling energized and motivated, and add more of those to your diet. Typically these will be the foods that have been tampered with the least, especially fresh veggies and fruits. Our bodies are designed to run on fuel that is most naturally accessible to us. Take a mental journey back to an earlier existence of human beings. We were primarily gatherers, gardeners, and hunters that consumed the food our environment was naturally able to support. We utilized as much of every food resource possible and maintained a relationship of gratitude with the land that provided for us.

Food provides us with the opportunity to thank our body for physically supporting our endeavors. Not only can we experience joy and relish in the flavor of the beautiful rainbow of natural foods, but are also able to practice self care. While sometimes this means indulging in decadence, it also means choosing the option that is better for our body long term. Every part of our body down to the tiniest cell reacts and responds differently dependent upon what foods you decide to put in your mouth. Before doing so, get into the habit of asking yourself, "Am I fueling wellness or disease?".

Making dietary changes is a continuous journey that requires dedication. Much of our choices are habitual, familial, or cultural in origin. We have limiting beliefs and ideas surrounding food just as we do in other areas of our life. I was intrigued to discover some of my own as my daughter began to eat solid foods. Intentionally exposing her to as many fresh foods as possible, I brought foods into the house that I was convinced I did not like. Upon serving them to her, I also wanted to exemplify these behaviors and began sampling (with admitted hesitation) these food items that I had dismissed long ago as "not for me". I gradually discovered that not only had my tastes changed since I'd made up my mind about a particular food, but many of those that I'd decided not to eat were ones that made me feel the best! Veggies were gradually becoming something that I'd look forward to enjoying the flavor of instead of turning up my nose at and picking them off of whatever they were baked or cooked into. Think about the foods you know would be beneficial for your body that you've decided you do not care for. How long ago did you classify them as such, and would it be worth revisiting? Try them different ways... perhaps cut into a meal you already know you love, or at different temperatures. Unless you've made a decision to cut a fresh food item out of your diet due to digestive reasons, your classification of this food is worth revisiting with an open mind.

Just as every person is unique, every digestive system is too. The current diet trend or dietary adjustments that may have worked well for a friend or family member may not be what is best for you. Keeping to a rigid diet plan that is the same for every family member may not work either, even if it contains foods that are natural and healthy. Our systems are also ever-changing and may need more or less of a certain food group even if this had been a good balance in the past.

For me personally, I have noticed a shift in the response to dairy over the last few years. As I'd mentioned previously, I grew up on a farm. While we were not a dairy farm, we had milk with every meal, as was traditional. I hold fond memories of my dad and I enjoying heaping bowls of ice cream together before bed on frequent occasions. Like most typical midwestern farming families, cheese was a part of many of the warm comfort meals that my mom so lovingly prepared.

My daughter is dairy-sensitive so I became more aware of what items contain small amounts of dairy and began preparing less of them. Since doing so I've begun to notice some signals my body has given me after consuming higher than average amounts of dairy... feelings I used to just accept as a part of life or a sign of eating too much. I'd feel excessively bloated, groggy, and irritable, and if I consumed enough my face would break out in a light rash of acne or dryness on my chin and sometimes the skin around my eyes.

At first I tried blaming my hormonal cycle, switched skin care routines, slathered on all the skin healing essential oils… basically trying with all my might to deny what I instinctively knew was the culprit. I quickly learned that a moment of enjoyment when eating, compared to a day or more of feeling out of sorts and not functioning at my highest potential was not always worth it. Sometimes a celebration or family gathering enables it to be enjoyable. My daily diet has shifted for the better since listening to and respecting my body.

Allow your intuition to guide you in creating meals and snacks that excite your senses while nourishing your body. As a society, we have experienced many changes in what is the "right" way to frame a meal or diet plan. From year to year and even month to month, the trends and recommendations change. One thing stays consistent… our intuition leading us in the right direction. While research and expert advice is to be considered, we also must understand that the responses of our own body trumps are to be held to the highest importance. Our own bodies are a much more reliable resource than that diet blog or nutritionist video, but we have to honor them enough to listen.

My older sister Amber spent several years in pain and mental fog. She experienced severe joint pain, especially in her hips, knees, and ankles. It was challenging to watch her, as a woman in her twenties, walk down the stairs as though she were many decades older… and even more challenging for her to experience. She noticed periods of time in which she felt she was in a "fog", unable to think clearly or function to the full height of her intelligence. When seeking answers from Western doctors and medical professionals she heard everything from "Fibromyalgia" to "Rheumatoid arthritis" and "Lupus". Feeling frustrated and unheard, she finally came across a doctor who encouraged that they work together. She understood that Amber was a scientist and college professor, and wanted to get to the bottom of this pain and suffering. She suspected her physical symptoms were diet related and began keeping a detailed food journal, keeping track of everything she consumed. Though it took some time, she finally discovered the root of the problem upon allowing herself to be led by her intuition. She was allergic to corn.

Amber realized the times in which she felt the worst corresponded with when she consumed foods with high amounts of corn-derived product in it. This corn allergy took awhile to catch onto, as many products contained an allergen that was not obvious. It was news to me that citric acid, natural flavor, or the use of cornstarch to keep food pieces from sticking together within packaging were all derived from this allergen. Since discovering her corn allergy, she has experienced the most beautiful transformation into a world of wellness. She feels better physically in her mid-thirties than she did in her early twenties and is able to show up for her son and the students in her classes as her alert self.

While every response is not as severe as this particular example (and some, more so), what we choose to put into our mouths and through our body initiates a response. Every food presents the opportunity to foster wellness or fuel disease… to create an environment of health or pain and inflammation. The more we can provide our body with the natural sustenance it needs, the more we are able to show up for ourselves and others in our daily lives.

How we are fueled transcends food and water alone. Just as we must avoid heavily processed and artificial foods and drinks, the consumption of content must be equally intentional. Think about how different media fuels your emotions and energy levels. Have you noticed certain news outlets or sources of information have the power to leave you feeling uplifted or fearful and disheartened? While we have a duty to be well-informed citizens, we also have the responsibility to protect our energy and maintain our own wellness. If watching the news leads to feelings of overwhelm and depression or following a particular person on social media results in the growth of your own limiting beliefs, adjust accordingly. Are the articles and stories you read and shows you watch leaving your feeling inspired and connected? Of course, we all will come across an array of content that invokes all sorts of emotion but we must actively seek to balance the negative with intentional positive. We have to intentionally listen to what our body is telling us and responding with love and compassion.

Fresh Air

We are living beings that thrive in nature… because we ourselves ARE nature. Receiving the original cure-all of fresh air, sunshine, and natural surroundings enables our soul to refresh. Imagine that every time you step outdoors surrounded by plants and trees, you are recharging your battery just as you do when you plug your phone into your outlet. Connecting with the trees and the native animals while breathing in fresh air is truly medicine to our mind, body, and spirit. Our brains are able to function at a higher capacity, our bodies are invited to be more active, and our soul can be refreshed by the soothing yet invigorating forces of nature.

Have you ever stepped outdoors, breathed deeply and felt, "ahhh, this is where I belong." Every element that can be experienced in nature around us is an external reflection of what can be felt within. We can hold the fury and intensity of a spring thunderstorm and the playful whimsy of a light breeze. Within our soul can be found the stability and sturdiness of a rock, the steady determination of a river. We can be as soft and gentle as the wings on a butterfly or as fierce and bold as a hunting lioness. Often we find ourselves intrigued by the natural forces that stir something deep in our soul... something familiar.

I once had a dream in which I was a part of a beautiful community of human beings. The vivid details of this comforting place have remained with me, as clear as a living memory. I recall a world in which kind humans lived as one with the natural world around them, with our little group residing in small treehouse style dwellings. These were not the rigid and boxy creations of modern treehouses. Instead, they blended into their surroundings as they were made from the very materials found in the densely forested area. My little treehouse cabin had only the simplest of items for daily life within, and was beautified with sprigs of herbs hanging to dry and flowers. I visited a friend by crossing a swaying bridge made from natural rope and sturdy sticks bound together, joining her own small space for tea and a chat among the birds and branches. The animals were unafraid of our presence, and it was obvious we lived harmonically with them in a world of mutual respect and unspoken understanding.

Upon waking I felt, "this must be a glimpse into what is considered heaven... nirvana… paradise." Unity, love, empathy, and a deep understanding that we do not visit nature but we come home to a place in which we belong. Just as the birds, animals, and trees of the forest are confident in their ways of being, we are encouraged to reunite with the natural world and feel the workings of spirit all around us. I remember feeling an ache, a longing for this familiar dream world while simultaneously understanding that in working toward a world such as this we may still have a chance at saving endangered species and natural habitats at risk of annihilation.

We are not separate from our environment. Our current societal priorities attempt to create this division between us and them. We are reminded that "nature" can be found within these park or restoration ground boundaries and everything beyond that is open for human inhabitants and destruction. By growing our empathy toward living beings beyond our own species and spending time outdoors while finding ways to bring the outdoors in, we are creating a place of residence for more than just our body. We are designing a home for our soul.

CHAPTER EIGHT:

C: Creative Expression & Connection

Creative Expression

Creativity is your intuition in action. Consider the last time you did something for yourself that lit you up, making you feel alive and full of inspiration. It is likely this activity had to do with creative expression! Empathic individuals thrive on creative expression regardless of whether one's chosen outlet is seen by your eyes alone or is held in the hands of thousands. Since empaths have a heightened intuitive understanding of others' feelings, we also are able to more naturally create art that evokes emotion. Often this is a subconscious act, one that flows naturally without consideration or premeditation. Other times you can feel the intent of the artist or creator clearly... often sharing messages of love, connection, or healing.

Some of you reading this may already be thinking, "Well, I'm not creative. I'm not artsy." If this is you I invite you to reassess with an open mind. You are alive, therefore you are here to create. Where some of us create paintings or music and otherwise traditionally considered "fine art" pursuits, others explore unique avenues of creative expression. Feng shui, macrame, cooking, designing lesson plans or courses, taking photos of your dog, and dancing around the kitchen to those nineties hits are all forms of creativity.

Expressing your emotion through whatever means available and inspiring to you is soul medicine, as it means you are tuning into your higher self and connection with the Universe. Your deep emotional capacities are not meant to be kept bottled up within. Move that energy, get those feelings out in healthy ways that leave you feeling refreshed. The right form of creative expression should leave you feeling as though you just left a counseling therapy with the most divine of therapists.

There was a point of transition in which I could feel my identity and intuitive connection begin to get a little lost again. It was a familiar feeling, as this time I was aware of what had happened before. I had recently made the decision to close my busy massage therapy office in order to spend more time at home with our daughter. While I still saw a small handful of clients as time allowed, I knew the art of healing was as good for me as it was for those on my table. However, I could already see the benefits of this decision reflected in our rapidly growing girl's eyes. A shift in my chosen creative outlet was needed. We regularly practiced yoga together, but time on the mat was joyfully becoming a less serene practice and more of a toddlers' human jungle gym. I needed something of my own that didn't have to wait until the early morning or late evening hours.

Enter macrame. I fell upon this creative hobby completely by accident. As my love of plants, natural fibers, and bohemian style grew, I looked to purchase a piece of macrame online. In true farm girl fashion I thought, "hm... I bet I can figure out a way to make this myself." And so I did. Borrowing a book from the library circa 1976 and making use of the wonderful tutorials available online, I created a simple plant hanger and wall hanging. I was hooked. The concentration required by the task at hand, the slow but steady visual progress, and the beautiful outcome most appreciated and understood by none other than myself was therapeutic. When feeling overwhelmed, lacking motivation, or just needing some space to clear my head in a productive way, those knots never failed to make me feel better.

Something happens when a person surrenders themselves to the creative process. Time passes differently. Worries and fears gently slip to the wayside. The mind is calmed by placing your mental energy on nothing but what you are creating, and your emotions are able to be worked through instead of settling in. Whether you're creating macrame art or a human life, the process of surrender to the intuitive powers that flow from you is magical. This is why musical scores can bring a person to tears... why gazing at a painting created by someone you've never met can make you feel a sense of comradeship with them... why the beauty of landscape architecture can give you chills.

Creation of all things from a place of true intuitive expression shakes others awake. It forms connection in those that may otherwise walk past noticing, but not truly seeing one another. Have you ever noticed the feeling of joyful comradery that takes place on a dance floor when a song is played that several people delight over? All of the sudden these people are brought together, experiencing a feeling of unity and understanding because of the creation and mutual appreciation of sounds strung together to form a melody and simple phonetic sounds resonating together as lyrics. Creative expression allows us to open our hearts and display our emotion in a raw and authentic way that often relates to the unspoken emotions of others.

To create is to be human… raw, open, present.

Connection (healthy)

We are wired to seek human connection and create bonds that allow us to feel safe and supported. Building connection and relationships is one thing, building healthy ones that foster your growth and development is quite another. Every person that comes into our life is in it for a reason, a purpose that the depths of which is rarely ever fully understood at the time.

Some are sent to trigger us… to make us feel frustrated and annoyed so we learn to step back and ask why. Every person that causes our anger to rise or resentment to develop is a flashing road sign pointing to areas that we have yet to heal or explore. We are then given the opportunity to venture down that road, exploring our shadows and observing the emotional responses that occur without allowing them to become our identity, nor our feelings to judge who the triggering person is at the core of their soul.

Others are full of unquestioned love and loyalty, and are bound to support you and your decisions no matter what. While these connections often feel good, grow our ego, and are often found within close familial bonds, they do not always allow room from true growth. If someone will knowingly turn a blind eye or even actively support something you know isn't the best for you, that is not healthy connection… that is an enabler.

Healthy connections are relationships with those who hold space for your thoughts, opinions, and feelings. While their beliefs may differ from your own, you are able to have open-minded discussions about them and consider new ideas together. You feel safe to be your true self and your intuition is trusted. There is little anxiety, worry, or fear regarding their connection and where you stand within it. Your body is relaxed, mind calm, and spirit refreshed in your time together. These connections, whether physically together daily or once every several years, are based upon a foundation of mutual respect. You see one another for the beautiful oneness human connection offers… the ability to see others as an extension of yourself interconnected within the web of life. This theory of "the human web" indicates that every human is at most six steps away from every other human on Earth in terms of "friend of a friend" and so on. Imagine going through life with the understanding your ripple of positive impact on the world simply by being a person of healthy connection for others.

While connecting with others in such a way is powerful, there is no more important healthy connection to have than with one's own self. Like many other highly intuitive beings, I've often sacrificed my own self love and care in order to make someone close to me feel more comfortable, at ease, or happy. Have you said things to yourself that you'd never say to a close loved one for fear of hurting them? Have you critiqued yourself more harshly than you'd consider judging your neighbor? Have you neglected building a healthy connection with yourself to help YOU grow because you've been so busy helping others?

You're not alone, and it's not too late. Building a relationship with yourself with a foundation of trust, respect, and compassion is not much different than fostering one with another human being. It requires consistency in trusting your intuition and demonstrating this with your decisions made. This healthy connection with one's self is grown through dedicating time and energy to your relationship. That's right, it's time to value your relationship with yourself as highly as (and eventually higher than) your relationship with others. At the end of your life it will matter most how YOU felt about the life you have lived, whether it was experienced to the fullest and if your unique love was shared as deeply as you knew you were able. Of the many connections you will create in your lifetime, the one with yourself is of highest value and importance.

Meditation prompt: Reconnect with yourself. Go for a coffee date, and instead of meeting up with a friend, bring along your journal. Spend some time walking in a nearby park or nature reserve. Leave the dishes for later and use nap time or your work break to reflect in peace, remaining open to intuitive guidance and spiritual wisdom.

SURVIVE & THRIVE KIT

CHAPTER NINE:

ENERGY PROTECTION & ALIGNMENT METHODS

The life habits to be a Mighty Force of Compassion will serve to create a foundation of aligned and protected energy. But we are all souls within a human experience, presenting itself with challenges where we could use a little extra assistance in doing so. The first is something that comes so naturally that we rarely take the time to think about it... your breath.

Deep Breathing

Your breathing does more than provide your cells with oxygen. The act of breathing has a direct relationship with our nervous system. When our nervous system is in a threatened state of danger, real or fabricated by the mind, our breathing rate shifts. We physiologically prepare ourselves to defend or escape. Unfortunately, this nervous system friend of ours does not distinguish between a physical threat such as a massive lion roaring only a few feet in front of you in the African plains and an emotional or mental threat, like your upcoming project deadline or handling conflict within your family. In either case, we are tensing up our muscles and taking more shallow breaths as our body fills with the "stress hormone" cortisol and adrenaline (the hormone epinephrine).

The incredible thing about the nervous system is the power to change the direction of this cycle as quickly as you can play the "reverse" card in a game of Uno. You can reverse this effect and enable the release of endorphins. Instead of tensing our body and preparing it for a fight or flight reaction we have the power to provide our body with the "feel good" hormone simply by deep breathing. This naturally produced chemical invites us to slow down and feel more relaxed, understanding that there are no immediate threats. It has even been scientifically proven to relieve pain.

Just by breathing.

The key here is obviously not the breathing itself. We have all felt the instant relaxation flooding over us from taking a soothing breath all of the way into the depths of our lungs. It brings with it an invigorating reminder of being alive. The key is remembering to do so before your nervous system has a chance to send those cards in the other direction. To catch yourself as you are amping up… as you begin to feel your anxiety rising or face flush with anger, and instead of jumping right to the reaction, pause. Rarely does a situation require such an immediate reaction, and by placing a pause for breath within the interaction you are able to separate yourself from the contradicting energy. Whatever the trigger was that began to take hold is recognized for what it is, and you have a perfect moment in time to separate yourself and your energy from that of the trigger. In leiu of becoming the emotion, you recognize the emotion outside yourself. Instead of joining the energy, you observe it and retain your own.

At times when you are already aware of your state of heightened emotion and seek to return to a place of peace or acknowledge in adance that the environment may cause such a state, you can bring along with you the invisible remedy of breathing exercises. One of my favorite breathing exercises to do is very effective at reducing the levels of stress hormones in the body, is proven to heighten concentration and focus, and is even used by Olympic athletes and U.S. Navy Seals. It is simple to do and is called square breathing or box breathing.

Meditation prompt: Begin by picturing a square, illuminated with a soft glow. Inhale slowly and deeply for four counts through the nose, hold that breath deep within your lungs for four counts, exhale slowly for four, and hold the exhale for four. With every inhale envision the fresh, cleansing energy entering your body... much like that first spring day where the smell in the air has shifted and you cannot help but fling open the windows. As you hold the breath in, picture the vibrance and refreshment of that breath illuminating and recharging every cell in your body. Exhale visualizing your worries, stresses and fears leaving your body with the breath out from your mouth. Holding the exhale, see the clutter or lower vibration energy these emotions carried floating off into the wind, no longer within your own energy field.

Visualizations

Just as you used visualizations as a part of your last meditation prompt, you can envision certain scenarios to assist in protecting your energy from negative attacks. Whether these attacks occur intentionally or not, visualizing your own energy field (if you aren't already able to see it) can be a helpful method of doing so. How you do so is completely up to you. Feel free to connect with your intuition to help guide you in your visualizations.

Imagery that helps me to feel safe and protected is the visualization of a bubble of golden light surrounding me. This divine bubble around me enabled me to see and reach out to help others, but does not allow lower vibrational energy attacks to permeate the boundary. If someone was saying something unkind, or taking part in activities that I would typically feel may harm my energy field I could watch with my mind's eye as these attacks bounced off my golden energy bubble! Some people enjoy envisioning the rainbow colors of their chakras or an army of angels surrounding them. Others may go through a little morning mime routine of zipping up their energy in the morning like a sleeping bag or cozy sweatshirt. Still others may choose to smooth their energy as though a bird with ruffled feathers. While there are countless ways to visualize your energy field or envision a scenario that calms you, I cannot choose these for you. Your mental and energetic space must be decorated by you, for you are the only one who can fully understand what calms you and resonates most strongly.

Sacred Space

Just as we create a space of energetic protection and safety within our mind, why not create one in our physical world as well? The energy felt and spaces created throughout your community and beyond is only minorly in your control. You can choose the environments in which you spend your free time, but you do not always have a choice over the neighbor's decor or your office's paint color. The environment you create in the space you have to do so can be a safe haven of rest and relaxation in an otherwise chaotic world. You may not know what types of energy you may come across throughout your day, but creating a sacred space in your home or place of residence assures you that when the day is done you will find peace.

There are many ways to do so and your living situation may lend a hand in how you go about the creation of your sacred space. You may set up a corner of your room, a shelf, or even dedicate an entire room (the bedroom is a wonderful one) to a place of calm and meditation. Like your mental visualizations, the physical space you set up must be set up for you, by you. First, clear the space of debri and clutter.

Preferably, empty it entirely and cleanse it energetically with sage (more about smudging with sage in the next chapter) or naturally derived cleaning products.

Only bring items into the space that are intentional and serve a purpose of either mind, body, or spirit. Perhaps a comfortable chair, stool, bolster, or rug for meditation, and a few plants or other earthy items that represent the different elements of nature. Something that reminds you of a powerful spiritual or energetic experience that you've had... a reminder of your spirit guides, soothing art, toxin-free candles, crystals, and books that hold enlightened wisdom for your life are all items that you may find to heighten the experience of your sacred space. Make it your haven of peace within a little corner of your soul manifested into reality. Then use this space for your prayers, meditation, yoga practice, journaling, creating, and simply being.

Mantra

Within your sacred space and anywhere you go in the world, you can choose to bring with you a mantra that helps you to attract and manifest your reality. Mantras do not have to be complicated, but are a simple sentence or phrase that brings you peace and helps you return to a place of connection with your intuition and higher self. Your mantra may be as short and simple as, "Be still" or a sentence of greater breadth such as "My life flows in divine synchronicity with love and light." A mantra can be chosen as your life motto that reminds you to navigate your life as your own… a life of integrity, bravery, love, and compassion.

Earthing

A practice referred to as earthing invites us to connect with the Earth with direct skin contact. Generations before received this naturally, where our modern society requires that we intentionally set aside time to do so. We've all felt the relaxing benefits of wandering our yard barefoot, but did you know there are scientific studies that support doing so? Whether our feet, hands, or another part of our body, connecting with the Earth directly enables mobile free electrons from the Earth to spread into our body. This foundational act of grounding our body with the Earth has been shown to improve sleep, boost the immune system, speed healing, and lower stress and blood pressure. While we addressed the benefits of spending time outdoors when discussing the Fresh Air habit of living as a Mighty Force of Compassion, developing a regular and intentional earthing practice allows you to take it to a heightened level.

Create & Enforce Healthy Boundaries

Establishing and abiding by healthy boundaries is a powerful way to protect your energy and prevent your compassionate nature from being taken advantage of. Whether in your work/life balance or relationships, family connections or personal decisions, creating healthy boundaries sets a framework for energy protection. If you aren't sure where or when to set boundaries, pay close attention to how you feel when your unspoken boundaries are crossed. When do you feel depleted or taken advantage of? These are clues as to areas of your life that could benefit from setting boundaries. Perhaps you require one day a week to enjoy some solitude and work on personal projects. Maybe you decide not to allow a toxic individual into the sacred space of your home. When you notice these tendencies to over-reach or over-extend yourself, take note of them and your newly discovered boundaries in your journal.

Recognizing the need for and creating these boundaries is only the first step while enforcing them is a lifelong commitment. You are allowed to say no to activities and extra opportunities to help others that don't feel right to you at any particular moment. If you feel the need to groan and say it is something you "should do", or "have to do"... reconsider your involvement. This also enables you to say yes whole-heartedly when presented with an idea or project that lights you up inside.

It is important to remember that these boundaries may change as time, your needs, and your environment shifts. Someone who was once in a place in which their companionship was not good for the soul may grow to become a healthy connection. In a prior phase of life you may have required more or less sleep to maintain a healthy energy balance. Just as life ebs and flows, your need for boundaries in different areas of it will change too. Check in with your intuitive wisdom and emotional responses in creating, enforcing, and updating your boundaries as they will never steer you wrong.

Energy Healing

As I described in an earlier chapter, energy medicine had such a powerful effect on my healing journey that I felt called to become a practitioner. Just as we receive a massage for physical tension relief or meditate to ease mental stress, energy healing is a healing art that works with the energetic body. Consider a time you've spent in natural waters… perhaps wading in the ocean, splashing along the banks of a river, or swimming in a beautiful lake. Did the water seem to refresh you in a way baths are unable to? While you may have still needed a shower, you were cleansing your energetic body and likely felt a renewed sense of self after emerging from the natural water.

Described by a friend as "a massage for the soul", energy healing awakens your intuition, helps you to feel balanced and aligned, and invites you to heal parts of you that may not be explored through Western Medicine pathways. In correcting disturbances of energy flow within and surrounding the body, energy healers are able to help patients overcome illnesses, injuries, and imbalances. These alternative modalities of healing are becoming increasingly mainstream, as global consciousness continues to rise and more people awaken to the possibility of deeper holistic healing. There are several different types of energy healing worth exploring, but here are a few notable modalities to look into. Take your time and try only one or two at a time, fully experiencing the unique process each ancient healing art has to offer.

- Acupuncture

Acupuncture is a process of inserting very thin needles into the skin at strategic locations. This type of energy healing is traditional Chinese medicine in which a practitioner relies on the understanding of the meridians, energy pathways throughout the body. In applying the needles to particular points, the practitioner is helping the patient to treat pain, encourage relaxation, and restore a healthy flow of energy or life force known as "chi" or "qi" (pronounced "chee").

- Reiki

Reiki is a Japanese technique of energy work that promotes relaxation, stress relief, and healing sometimes referred to as the "laying on of hands". A Reiki practitioner channels healing universal life force energy by gently placing their hands on or just above a patient's body. In doing so the patient's natural healing energy is activated enabling physical healing, feelings of emotional well-being, and spiritual peace and guidance to occur.

- Aromatherapy

Aromatherapy utilizes essential oils, or the essence of plants, to positively affect the energetic body. Just as we burn sage to clear a space or person of negative energy, authentic plant-derived oils can be used to heal and protect an individual's energy field. Oils such as frankincense and rosemary are referred to in multiple historic and spiritual texts, demonstrating the pertinence of essential oils in spiritual cleansing, healing, and growth. An aromatherapist uses a minute amount of pure essential oil, typically combined with a carrier oil to safely dilute the potent oil. The oils may be chosen to heal a particular energy center, aid in the rebalancing of hormones, or invite stress relief and relaxation.

- Sound Healing

This modality of energy work uses the healing vibrations created by the reverberation of sound for relaxation and health benefits. Certain frequencies of sound have been discovered to help speed healing and deepen relaxation. From a cat's purr, to Tibetan or glass singing bowls, chanting, or meditation music created specifically for these purposes, the vibration of sound can be a powerful healer.

- Crystal Healing

Crystals have been used for healing and spiritual rituals since the beginning of time, and humans of all cultures wore or displayed them as a symbol of health and prosperity. Crystal healing is the use of semi-precious gemstones and crystals that occur naturally around the world. Different crystals emit different vibrational energy frequencies, making them beneficial for different areas of healing. For example, obsidian is used for grounding and root chakra healing while rose quartz activates positive energy, increases feelings of love (for self and others alike), and is used to align the heart chakra.

- Spiritual Intuitive, Spiritual Coaching, or Intuitive Counseling

Much like psychological counseling or talk therapy, an Intuitive converses with a client and helps them reconnect with their own intuition. They may receive aid in doing so from spiritual presence or simply their own empathic senses to guide them in understanding their own emotions and spiritual journey.

CHAPTER TEN:

PHYSICAL EMPATH TOOLKIT

I'd like to preface these suggestions with an important reminder. You can carry around every single one of these physical tools to protect your energy and support your empath journey but if you refuse to do the internal healing and growth, you will likely continue to struggle. The items I mention are wonderful tools but they are just that... tools. A woodworker may have the finest of tools but without the time, commitment, and knowledge behind them, their creations will likely be lackluster. Just as tools are not the determining factor of an outcome for woodworkers, empaths are not made wiser or vision more clear simply by the tools she or he chooses to use.

However... they sure can help!

Having something to physically hold on to, see, smell, or use can be a source of encouragement. Often these little helpers can be just the nudge we need to connect more deeply with our intuition and our purpose. From herbal medicine and crystal healing to spiritual rituals that have been around for centuries, we can receive support from the physical world around us. Focusing our attention on something other than our internal struggles or anxiety allows us to rebalance while feeling the benefits of nature's healing and ancestral wisdom.

Herbs, Teas & Essential Oils

Just as a diet containing fresh plants helps us to receive the nutritional balance we need, herbal teas can balance our emotions, regulate our hormones, and support our energetic health. Herbs and herbal teas have been used for centuries in spiritual ceremony and for medicinal healing purposes. There are many to learn about and choose from but here are some of the most commonly used and a few of the uses that make them most sought after:

- Chamomile

Chamomile is known for its relaxation properties and is often consumed or applied before bed to support healthy sleep cycles.

- Lavender

Lavender is also well-known for relaxation and as a sleep aid, as well as easing anxiety and depression.

- Peppermint

Peppermint can be used to stimulate mental focus and ease digestion.

- Lemon

Lemon is known for its cleansing properties, both outside and inside of the body. It helps to detox your cells and cleanse the liver.

- Sage

Sage is a spiritual and energetic purifier, and rids one of negative energies.

- Turmeric

Turmeric is known to reduce inflammation, making it a great pain reliever.

- Rosemary

Rosemary improves cognitive function and focus, as well as reducing inflammation.

- Frankincense

Frankincense is helpful for opening the third eye, for meditation and spiritual growth.

- Eucalyptus

Eucalyptus helps to open the airways and clear the respiratory system, as well as promoting relaxation.

- Lemongrass

Lemongrass can help to reduce fever, and relieve pain and swelling.

- Fennel

Fennel is known to increase milk supply in nursing women, support healthy female reproductive health and digestion, and aid in regulating blood pressure.

While this list includes just the basics, there is much to be explored and discovered in using herbs and essential oils, and drinking herbal teas for yourself personally. Herbal remedies are a natural way to understand your own body's rhythms and cycles more thoroughly, and trust Mother Nature and our intuition.

Epsom Salt Bath

A personal favorite to enjoy at the end of a turbulent day, soaking in a warm bath with a half cup of epsom salts can assist in cleansing your energetic body. It is believed that the combination of magnesium and sulfate works to increase the body's natural detoxification process, helps to promote the release of melatonin (the sleep hormone), and relaxes the muscles. Personally I've been able to achieve some of my deepest meditative states, including the meeting of my spirit guides, when relaxed in an Epsom Salt bath. The experience can feel as though your entire energetic body, not just your physical one, is cleansed and refreshed.

Bolsters, Mats, & Blocks

If you are taking up a regular meditation or yoga practice, you may benefit from the use of a few physical assistance items. Bolsters or meditation cushions can be helpful for allowing you to relax your mind by inviting your body to be more at ease. They can assist you in restorative poses and simply be a comfortable place to sit or lie upon when meditating. A yoga mat can be helpful to add a small amount of cushion between you and the ground and floor. This eases the pressure put on joints and enables you to more comfortably ease into poses or peacefully relax into meditation. The material helps to increase your grip, preventing you from losing your balance due to an overly smooth or slippery surface. Yoga blocks are as close as you can get to having a yoga instructor helping you reach more challenging poses, supporting you where you need it, and deepening your stretch. They can also be wonderful for helping you ease into restorative postures, just as a bolster does but with more firmness.

Crystals

Crystals and stones have been revered throughout history to have mystical powers. Whether worn as jewelry, collected as decor, or used in energy healing, crystals of the world have ignited feelings of curiosity and awe. There's no question that human beings have been enamored with the beauty of crystals, but how do they help?

The alternative healing field of crystal healing can be powerful to empaths. Where one person may not feel or experience the vibrational healing found in the world of crystals, someone with heightened energetic perceptions may feel deeply cleansed and refreshed by them. Here are a few ways crystals may help you:

- Worry stones/pocket crystals

Keeping a crystal in your pocket or even choosing one that has been shaped into a "worry stone" are soothing to hold between your fingers. Worry stones are any that have been polished into a curved oval shape that is calming to hold and rub between the thumb and forefinger. Typically slender, they are easy to slip into a pocket or purse and use inconspicuously during times of anxiety, nervousness, or stress.

- Jewelry

Gemstones and semi-precious gems can be worn as jewelry on the body to help protect and refresh your energy. A visual reminder of your intent and vibrational support and protection, these decorative items can adorn you for a deeper purpose than simply accessorizing an outfit.

- Prayer/Mala/Meditation beads

Throughout many major religions or spiritual beliefs, beads of gems or semi-precious gems have been used to aid the mind in focusing on our prayer or meditation. Each bead may symbolize a particular prayer, be a repetition of your mantra, or extend an invitation to reflect with gratitude on the many people and experiences to be grateful for in our lives.

Cards

Whether you feel most comfortable trying affirmation cards, oracle cards, or tarot cards, these decks are simple ways to allow your intuition and connection to the Universe to easily come through. By choosing a card to help guide your intentions for the day, or in asking support for a situation in which you are struggling, you are able to receive a simple phrase or image (sometimes both) to point you in the right direction or reframe your ways of thinking.

Sage Bundles & Palo Santo

Whether looking to cleanse and refresh your own energy or that of your surroundings, burning sage is a popular way to do so that dates back hundreds of years. Sage is an aromatic herb that has been used throughout many cultures to prevent illness, cleanse and heal, repel insects and negative energies, and in spiritual rituals and ceremonies. This herb is easy to grow and dry yourself, or you can find bundles of sage at your local reiki, crystal, or mystical shops and even some health food or farmers markets. While there are many varieties of sage, white sage is most commonly used and is associated with purity. Palo Santo is a wood that serves a similar purpose of cleansing and removing negative energies from a space or person.

Anytime you're able to give the process your full attention is a good time to burn sage or Palo Santo, but especially when moving into a new space, after an illness, argument, or negative occurrence. You can also do so during meditation to invite in high vibration spiritual guidance. I personally enjoy cleansing my energetic body with either in conjunction with an epsom salt bath and meditation, and always feel deeply refreshed and uplifted after ridding myself of negative emotions or experiences. There are five simple steps in doing so.

1. Before you begin, remember to be mindful and respectful of such an ancient tradition that is spiritual in nature to many cultures, especially that of native tribes. Burn your sage or wood with honor and gratitude for this healing plant and Mother Earth. Thank your spiritual guides for being present with you and assisting with your cleansing and healing. Open windows where you are intending to cleanse, if even just a crack. Prepare your ritual items with care.

2. Set clear intentions as you light a candle. You may repeat these intentions out loud or to yourself as you move about your home or cleanse yourself. This can be something simple such as, "I cleanse this space of negative energy that does not belong here. I invite only love to enter here" or can be as complex and specific as you'd like. Just follow your intuition in doing so!

3. After setting your intentions, light the leafy end of your sage stick or bundle with your candle. Allow it to burn for a few moments before extinguishing the flame. Bringing along a small fireproof (ceramic or glass) bowl or abalone shell, begin at the front door of your home or space. Waft the smoke into all corners of the space using your hand or a feather. Be mindful of cupboards, closets, and dark corners that often receive little fresh energy flow. Repeat your intention or mantra as you move clockwise around your home.

4. To smudge yourself, use a feather, fan, or simply your hand and "wash" the smoke over your body. Different sources may tell you to begin at your head, heart, or at your feet, but the most important thing is to breathe deeply, tune into your body, and repeat your intentions. Enjoy the soothing smoke while connecting with your higher power.

5. To extinguish, do so in sand, on the earth, or a ceramic dish. Do not use water. Notice and enjoy your space (and yourself) feeling lighter, fresher, and more pure. Give thanks and invite love, light and pure energy in!

Affirmations

Affirmations, much like mantras, are intentionally chosen words to positively impact your health and wellness. Think of them as little messages of encouragement or reassurance to yourself, helping to rid your mind of limiting beliefs while replacing them with intentional ones. Using affirmations regularly enables you to shift your mindset and manifest the reality you wish to create. You can choose to repeat them during your meditation, tell yourself your affirmations in the mirror every morning, or write little notes to place around your home where you will see them most!

Books

I urge you to never stop expanding your mind and opening your heart to new ideas, so long as they further the spread of love and empathy and advance your growth. Read books about subjects you receive a glimmer of curiosity about, topics that trigger you, and self-help support in pursuing your passions. Books enable you to acquire knowledge from a diverse group of people, living and dead, who have a message to share. Having written one, I can tell you that no one goes through the process of doing so without commitment to sharing their message and the understanding that what they have to share is important and life-changing for someone. Perhaps millions, perhaps a small handful of individuals… but you never know if you are one of them until you pick up their book and read.

We live in a time in which books have never been more accessible. Whether instantly downloadable onto your electronic device, narrated on your favorite app, or shipped to your door in a matter of days, you are able to access a world of knowledge without ever leaving your home. Libraries around the country are able to borrow and share books that are not already on their shelves, and we are able to discuss books we have gained insight from with people around the world in real time. Here are a few authors I recommend learning from:

- Eckhart Tolle
- Deepak Chopra
- Gabrielle Bernstein
- Brene Brown
- Judith Orloff
- Tara Brach
- Abraham Hicks

CHAPTER ELEVEN:

BE OF SERVICE

My dear empath friend,

I'm grateful you decided to come along on this journey with me, as it is one that will lead you to a life of deepened fulfillment and wellness. You are now faced with a choice. You can consider this book to be one to check off the list, one you've taken a couple of stories to heart from or perhaps quote once or twice...

Or...

You can join the movement of healers, artists, teachers, and guides working toward a better world together. You are not alone in your sensitivity and you most certainly aren't alone on this path of empath healing and growth. Allow the moments of internal clarity and peace to be a catalyst of change within your own habits and lifestyle that permeate far beyond your four walls. You are a force to be reckoned with, a Mighty Force of Compassion. Let this compassion within your heart and knowledge of how to care for yourself spread like wildfire by sharing, but more importantly, by exemplifying what it means to be an empath capable of joining forces to heal this world. It won't always be easy. In fact, there will be days you question this journey with every ounce of your being. There will be breakthrough tears and trauma brought to the surface that you were unaware even existed. You will uncover ancestral pain and see through societal systems created to maintain divisiveness and greed. You may see friends fade away and witness a few people close to you resist your newly discovered and implemented boundaries.

Yet through these challenges you are given the opportunity to find yourself. Your true, unbridled and free to express, joyful and abundant, empathic self. You may have stumbled along this discovery on your own... after all, I know your intuition is capable of guiding you there... but now you have a guidebook, a reference to seek wisdom and direction from. Not only this, but a community of welcoming and supportive individuals cheering you on along the way. Join us on Instagram and Facebook (using hashtags #empathsattheedge and #beamightyforceofcompassion) and inquire about events in your area.

You are not only capable, you are destined for a beautiful life full of magic and oneness. So take this knowledge and practice it. Apply the concepts to your daily life one step at a time, giving yourself the time and space to adjust and checking in with your higher self along the way. Here are some ideas of how to do so, taking this book from words on a page or screen to actions within a peacefully aligned life:

- Hold a book club, empath circle, or sensitivity support group using this book as a framework to learn from one another's experiences.

- Go back through and highlight ideas, habits, and changes that you know would benefit you and implement them one at a time, adding a new one each week.

- Discuss the things you've learned with someone close to you who you are already aware has heightened empathic sense and abilities.

- Keep an extra book, notepad, or affirmation cards in your car, bag, or wallet, ready to share when you happen upon a friend or stranger in need of an uplifting message of support and encouragement.

By growing through your struggles, challenges, and fears you have an incredible opportunity to help others. The very experiences that have created dark times within your life were there to teach your light how to shine even brighter. You are made more beautiful and your story more relatable by your scars. However you choose to do so, you have the ability to help others going through similar struggles to light the way. We heal ourselves by paving the way of enlightened navigation through your own journey. We invite others to heal by turning back and illuminating the very path we've paved.

There is a Japanese art by the name of Kintsugi in which a broken object of pottery is repaired. Instead of being tossed aside, the pieces of a broken dish are repaired with a lacquer that is dusted or mixed with gold, silver, or platinum. This pottery is made even more beautiful with the care in which it is repaired. Your areas of pain and feelings of brokenness do not deem you unusable... quite the contrary! Allow yourself the grace to apply a lacquer of gold with self love to those raw edges in need of healing and repair. In doing so you are joining together your story with beauty that creates a masterpiece far stronger, more unique, and vibrant than before.

Thank you for being brave enough to explore within. Give yourself gratitude for opening your heart and mind to the wisdom meant for you. May this be a launching point from the edge to soaring into a life fulfilled with love, peace, and empathic service.

With love and light,

Ashley Kay Andy

REFERENCES

Alcantara, Margarita. *Chakra Healing: A Beginner's Guide to Self-Healing Techniques that Balance the Chakras.* Berkeley, California: Althea Press, 2017

Aron, Elaine. *The Highly Sensitive Person.* New York, NY: Harper Thorsons, 2017

Chevalier, Gaétan et al. "Earthing: health implications of reconnecting the human body to the Earth's surface electrons." *Journal of environmental and public health vol. 2012* (2012): 291541. doi:10.1155/2012/291541

Cuda, Gretchen. "Just Breathe: Body Has A Built-In Stress Reliever" NPR, 6 December 2010

Dutt, Nabanita. What Is A Spiritual Bath – And Why You Should Try One To Help Bring Positive Changes Into Your Life. Accessed 13 July, 2020. https://hydralivetherapy.com/blog/2019/07/24/2019-6-28-what-is-a-spiritual-bath-and-why-you-should-try-one-to-help-bring-positive-changes-into-your-life/

Easley, Thomas. Horne, Steven The Modern Herbal Dispensatory: A Medicine-Making Guide. Berkeley, California. North Atlantic Books, 2016

Kahlsa, Shakta Kaur. *Yoga for Women.* London: United Kingdom: DK, 2007

McNeil, J.R. McNeil, William. *The Human Web: A Bird's-Eye View of World History.* New York, NY: W. W. Norton & Company, 2003

Navarro, Tomas. *Kintsugi: Embrace Your Imperfections and Find Happiness the Japanese Way.* London, United Kingdom: Yellow Kite, 2018

Orloff, Judith. "The Top Ten Traits of an Empath." Accessed 23 May 2020. https://drjudithorloff.com/top-10-traits-of-an-empath

Rosen, Rebecca. "Intuition 101: Developing Your Clairsenses." Accessed June 3, 2020. http://www.oprah.com/spirit/developing-your-5-clair-senses-rebecca-rosen/all

Singer, Michael. *The Untethered Soul: The Journey Beyond Yourself.* Oakland, California: New Harbinger Press, 2013

Rodika Tchi. *The Healing Power of Smudging: Cleansing Rituals to Purify Your Home, Attract Positive Energy and Bring Peace into Your Life.* Berkeley, California: Ulysses Press, 2017

Winfrey, Oprah, host. "Best Lifesaving Lessons." Oprah's SuperSoul Conversations, 31 July 2019. https://omny.fm/shows/oprah-s-supersoul-conversations/best-lifesaving-lessons

Made in the USA
Las Vegas, NV
29 March 2022